GRAPHIC DESIGN FOR FASHION
JAY HESS AND SIMONE PASZTOREK

LAURENCE KING PUBLISHING

LAURENCE KING

Published in 2010 by
Laurence King Publishing Ltd
361–373 City Road
London EC1V 1LR
Tel: +44 20 7841 6900
Fax: +44 20 7841 6910
e-mail: enquiries@laurenceking.com
www.laurenceking.com

Published in 2010 by Laurence King Publishing Ltd

A catalogue record for this book is available from the British Library

ISBN: 978 1 85669 693 7

Design: ByBoth
Senior editor: Peter Jones
Photography: PSc Photography www.pscphotoltd.co.uk

Printed in China

INVITATIONS

BRANDING

LOOKBOOKS

PACKAGING

INTRODUCTION

THE CREATIVE PROCESS CAN BE DISTILLED INTO A SERIES OF BINARY DECISIONS – YES OR NO, ON OR OFF, GOOD OR BAD. WHILE A MOMENT OF INSPIRATION CAN TAKE AN IDEA IN A NEW DIRECTION, THE SAME CYCLE OF EVALUATION IS REQUIRED TO GIVE SHAPE TO THE CONCEPT. THE REFINEMENT OF THESE OPTIONS IS ULTIMATELY EXTREMELY PERSONAL. EVEN THE MOST OBJECTIVE APPROACH STILL REQUIRES SUBJECTIVE EDITING OF THE POSSIBILITIES. THE PERSONAL NATURE OF THIS PRACTICE CREATES IMMEDIATE TENSION WHEN CREATIVITY BECOMES A COMMODITY.

THE GRAPHIC DESIGNER OCCUPIES THIS DIFFICULT **POSITION WITH GROWING CONFIDENCE. WITH THE ADVANCE IN TECHNOLOGY, VISUAL COMMUNICATION HAS BECOME MORE SOPHISTICATED AND PERVASIVE. AS THE SOCIAL IMPACT OF GRAPHIC DESIGN INCREASES, ITS RESPONSIBILITY NOW REACHES BEYOND TRADITIONAL PRINTED MATTER INTO BRAND MANAGEMENT AND DIGITAL MEDIA. WHILE SELF-INITIATED PROJECTS PROVIDE AN ADDITIONAL CREATIVE OUTLET FOR THE STUDIO, THE CORE BUSINESS OF GRAPHIC DESIGN REMAINS THE COMMERCIAL SERVICE OF CLIENTS. THE STRENGTH OF THIS PARTNERSHIP – BETWEEN DESIGNER AND CLIENT – IS FUNDAMENTAL TO**

THE SUCCESS OF EACH PROJECT. HOW WOULD THE DYNAMIC OF THE RELATIONSHIP CHANGE WITH AN EQUALLY CREATIVE CLIENT?

THERE IS AN INCREASED SENSE OF CREATIVE POTENTIAL WHEN THE GRAPHIC DESIGN STUDIO IS COMMISSIONED BY THE FASHION INDUSTRY. SYNONYMOUS WITH VISUAL AND CONCEPTUAL INNOVATION, FASHION IS ALSO GROUNDED IN COMMERCIAL REALITIES. THE BENEFITS OF A MORE INTEGRATED CREATIVE RELATIONSHIP WITH FASHION WERE NOT FULLY REALISED UNTIL PETER SAVILLE WAS COMMISSIONED FOR THE AUTUMN/WINTER 1986/87 LOOKBOOK FOR YOHJI YAMAMOTO. HIS COLLABORATION WITH ART DIRECTOR MARC ASCOLI AND PHOTOGRAPHER NICK KNIGHT BECAME THE DEFINING MOMENT OF MODERN FASHION COMMUNICATION. ALMOST IMMEDIATELY, 'GRAPHICS' BECAME AS VITAL FOR FASHION AS IT HAD BEEN FOR THE MUSIC INDUSTRY.

THE CREATIVE FREEDOM INVOLVED IN WORKING WITH THE FASHION INDUSTRY HAS MADE THE RELATIONSHIP HIGHLY DESIRABLE FOR GRAPHIC DESIGNERS. THE CYCLICAL FASHION SEASONS PROVIDE CONSISTENT OPPORTUNITY FOR REINVENTION AND RARELY PRODUCE LESS THAN SPECTACULAR RESULTS. THIS FREEDOM OFTEN DIRECTLY INFLUENCES THE BROADER PRACTICE

OF THE DESIGN STUDIO: FASHION CAN BECOME A UNIQUE CREATIVE PLAYGROUND FOR EXPERIMENTATION WITHIN THE COMMERCIAL WORLD.

BROKEN INTO FOUR CHAPTERS OF BRANDING, INVITATIONS, LOOKBOOKS AND PACKAGING, THE FOLLOWING PAGES ARE AN INTERNATIONAL SURVEY OF CONTEMPORARY GRAPHIC DESIGN AND FASHION. ADVERTISING AND DIGITAL MEDIA REPRESENT AN ALTERNATIVE BEYOND THE CORE SKILLS OF THE GRAPHIC DESIGNER. ALL PROJECTS FEATURED IN THESE PAGES FOCUS ON THE MAIN LINE COLLECTIONS BEFORE ANY ACCESSORY LINES OR BEAUTY PRODUCTS.

MORE THAN A SHOWCASE, THE BOOK PROVIDES THE CONTEXT SURROUNDING THE WORK, AND THE RESULT IS A COLLECTIVE DIALOGUE ABOUT THE RELATIONSHIP AND PRACTICE OF THE WORLD'S LEADING GRAPHIC DESIGNERS AND FASHION DESIGNERS. CREATIVE ENTHUSIASM AND A COMMON VISUAL LANGUAGE CAN BE A MUTUAL BENEFIT BUT THERE ARE NO PREREQUISITES, RULES OR GUARANTEES FOR A CONSTRUCTIVE OR INNOVATIVE RELATIONSHIP. AS WITH CREATIVITY IN GENERAL, IT IS FIRST AND FOREMOST A PERSONAL DECISION-MAKING PROCESS.

ACKNOWLEDGEMENTS

WE ARE GRATEFUL FOR THE TIME, EFFORT AND ENTHUSIASM THAT ALL OF THE CONTRIBUTORS HAVE BROUGHT TO THIS PROJECT.

WE APPRECIATE THE OPPORTUNITY TO PRODUCE THIS BOOK FOR LAURENCE KING, IN PARTICULAR THE TRUST SHOWN BY HELEN ROCHESTER, THE DETERMINATION OF PETER JONES AND THE SAINTLY PATIENCE OF SIMON WALSH.

THROUGHOUT THE PROCESS WE RECEIVED WORDS OF ADVICE AND ENCOURAGEMENT FROM MARK GLASSNER, KEVIN VUCIC SHEPARD, MALU HALASA, ANDY COX, HYWEL DAVIES AND OF COURSE MANFRED AND LUISE PASZTOREK.

THE TIRELESS EFFORT THAT WENT INTO THE PHOTOGRAPHY OF THE BOOK HAS SURPASSED OUR EXPECTATIONS. MANY THANKS TO STEVE SMITH AND THE WHOLE TEAM AT PSc PHOTOGRAPHY FOR THEIR SKILL AND ATTENTION TO DETAIL.

BRANDING

IS THE CONSCIOUS MANAGEMENT OF THE PUBLIC PERCEPTION OF, AND PERSONAL IDENTIFICATION WITH, A FASHION LABEL.

INTRODUCTION

THERE IS A SIMPLICITY TO THE MOST EFFECTIVE BRANDING THAT BELIES ITS UNDERLYING COMPLEXITY. MORE THAN AN IDENTIFIABLE LOGO, BRANDING IS CONSIDERED A PROMISE, AN EXPERIENCE AND A MEMORY. THE MESSAGE MUST COMMUNICATE THE AMBITION OF THE LABEL AND THE PERSONAL AND SOCIAL BENEFITS OF ASSOCIATION. THE NATURE OF FASHION ELEVATES ASPIRATION ABOVE AUTHENTICITY. COMPETITION IS FIERCE AND GROWING: THE CONSUMER IS BOMBARDED WITH HUNDREDS OF BRANDED MESSAGES EVERY DAY. THE CHALLENGE LIES IN CONTROLLING THESE VERY INTANGIBLE ELEMENTS WITH VERY TANGIBLE MEANS.

HOW DO YOU KNOW WHEN SOMETHING IS GOOD?
THAT DEPENDS ON WHAT YOU WANT TO ACHIEVE.
BUT USUALLY SOMETHING IS GOOD IF YOU FEEL GOOD
ABOUT IT. IT'S A GUT FEELING[18]   I THINK IT'S THE
TOUGHEST THING OF BEING CREATIVE: TO SEE WHEN
SOMETHING IS GOOD, TO SEE WHEN IT IS FINISHED.
BUT AT THE VERY MOMENT YOU REACH THIS POINT
YOU'LL FEEL IT. IT IS THE MOMENT WHEN EVERYTHING,
EVERY INGREDIENT OF YOUR CREATION IS IN TUNE.
IT FEELS LIKE ENLIGHTENING, A BEAUTIFUL, TENDER
MOMENT... AND AN EXTREME SATISFACTION...[26]
YOU NEVER KNOW, I THINK IT'S MORE A FEELING[30]
INTUITION[32]   I WOULD SAY IF THE IDEA YOU HAVE IS
TRANSLATED IN A DIRECT WAY. THE IDEA CAN ALSO
BE A VIEWPOINT. ASSUMING THE IDEA IS INTERESTING
TO BEGIN WITH. SPECIFIC IDEAS CAN LEAD TO NEW
AND INTERESTING FORMAL SOLUTIONS. ONCE THAT
HAPPENS YOU USUALLY KNOW IT IS GOOD[36]   WHEN
IT IS SUITABLE[44]   I THINK YOU CAN FEEL IT AND
PERHAPS VERY OFTEN I THINK YOU CAN FEEL IT
BEFORE IT IS FINISHED[50]   GUT FEELING[54]   IF THE
CONCEPT HAS A TWIST AND WE CONTINUE TO LIKE
THE PROJECT LONG AFTER IT WAS COMPLETED[56]

ACNE ART DEPARTMENT for
ACNE STUDIOS

Acne Art Department is an autonomous member of the multidisciplinary Acne collective, based in a single building on the cobbled streets of Gamla Stan, Stockholm. A unique and highly effective creative ecosystem, Acne is now comprised of seven companies, which provide internal expertise, while each independently pursues external clients and projects. Originally incorporated as part of Acne Creative, the specialization of advertising and graphic design was acknowledged in 2008 when Acne Advertising and Acne Art Department were established.

Acne is the acronym for 'Ambition to Create Novel Expression', and while this is a statement of intention, it also refers to a less than desirable skin condition, a potentially insurmountable obstacle for the image-conscious fashion industry. Through intelligent and innovative brand management, Acne Art Department have played a major role in overhauling this perception for the Acne Studios fashion brand. It has been so successful that a survey of university students in Stockholm found that the majority of them associate 'Acne' primarily with jeans, not skin problems.

Since the modest production of 100 pairs of unisex jeans for family and friends in 1998, Acne Studios have become synonymous with effortless style and sophistication. Their main challenge has always been to find a balance between artistic inclinations and commercial realities. The visual language has provided a vital foundation for their exponential global expansion. Acne Art Department have implemented a consistent communication programme, never losing sight of the brand ideals while supporting each stage of the evolution. "There is never an opportunity for us to explain to each and every consumer about why things look a certain way. For them, it just

does, and they have to like the result in order to want it," says art director Daniel Carlsten.

Central to the branding exercise is *Acne Paper*, a seasonal fashion magazine that is the flagship of Acne Studio's visual communication. Established in Autumn/Winter 2005/06, it supports the current collection, but also opens its pages up to rival labels. Although undoubtedly a piece of self-publicity, it promotes Acne Studios' inspiration and conceptual development rather than specific products and services. As a self-perpetuating creative loop, this provides a 'style guide' that informs and is fed into by all the members of the Acne family.

The benefits of working within the collective are invaluable. "There is incredible freedom and enormous trust. We have been able to treat Acne Studios like it was our own brand, and we have done things that we would like to see as consumers. This enables very intuitive work," says art director Jonas Jansson. Seeing themselves as customers strengthens the department's ability to distil the brand values with increased precision. This is particularly evident in the high take-up rate of their initial concepts.

Inspiration for the Acne Studios branding comes from within. "Working in the multidisciplinary collective of Acne where there are film production, advertising, web production, toy manufacturing and all kinds of different collaborative projects, we simply use the idea of Acne when creating the Acne brand," says Carlsten. "It's always a mix of ideas. It's fascinating when something ordinary is presented in an unexpected way or in an unexpected context. Not in an attempt to be weird for the sake of weird, but in the success of being surprisingly relevant."

"The fashion industry is sensitive to visual communication and understands and values its importance in order to create and develop a look, a feeling or a brand," says Jansson. "When working with other creatives, we are among friends. We are an integral part of the creative process and the product itself. We are creating fashion, yet not specific garments. Fashion is about packaging. We are creating fashion, in the sense that graphic design and art direction are an integral part of fashion."

To achieve such integration with clients requires more than a shared office. There is an eagerness to understand what motivates them, practically and aesthetically. While this process is infinitely easier with Acne Studios, the experience impacts directly on the department's broader practice. Art director Moses Voigt acknowledges the complexities of finding the balance with creative clients as they "often tend to use visuals, as opposed to a written brief, which can be a good thing, because words may be interpreted in so many ways. Interpretations open up misunderstandings. Pictures are more direct and easier to discuss." A shared visual language is a prerequisite to ensure the best results.

The easy exchange of ideas lies at the heart of Acne Art Department. Collaboration, or dialogue as Jansson has implied, is of constant importance in their collective working environment. Within such an open platform, certain practicalities need to be put in place to maintain consistency. "It is extremely inspiring working with talented, creative people, but sometimes someone needs to take charge." Managing creative expectations without crushing motivation can also be challenging. "Stubbornness is in itself not a goal, it just makes you a pain in the arse. There are always many solutions to a problem. We try to find one that everyone involved is happy with," says Jansson.

In modern society, fashion is more than the production of clothing. Acne Art Department have a strong understanding of the need to consistently maximize the potential of their clients' communication. With an acute self-awareness they blur the line between graphic designer, client and audience with great effect.

www.acneartdepartment.se
www.acnestudios.com

Acne Paper is a biannual fashion magazine launched in 2005. As an alternative to conventional print advertising, Acne Paper's initial purpose was as a vehicle to promote the brand aesthetic and act as a moodboard showcase of the creative inspiration of each season. It also provides a collaborative showcase for the whole 'family' under the Acne umbrella (Advertising, Art Department, Production, JR, and Fashion & Denim). Oversized at 28 x 38cm (11 x 15in) and printed on various coated and uncoated paper stocks, the content is intimate and direct, leaving the impression of having viewed a personal portfolio. A selection of covers is shown here, overleaf is an opening spread. The distinct and consistent typographic treatment is shown on page 24.

JEANS

OLIVER GOLDSMITH, Eyewear Designer

> "I saw great potential in my grandfather's and my father's business."
>
> Particularly in my father's designs, from which I created my own image for the 1960s."
>
> —Oliver Goldsmith

LOOK IE VER

SHELF PORTRAITS

Photographed by
BRENDAN AUSTIN

P 33
NADIA VAN 'T VEER, Photography Agent at UNIT

P 58 & 59
LANCE and ROBERT FENTWISTLE, Art Dealers

P 60-61
HASSAN ABDULLAH, MICHEL LASSERE and STEFAN KARLSSON,
Restaurateurs behind LES TROIS GARÇONS

P 63
GERT JONKERS, Founder and Editor of BUTT and FANTASTIC MAN

P 65
ANTONY MILES, Editor of to and to...

JOHN CANDON, Guitarist in SPIRITUALIZED

*This is a small selection of the vast array of
branding collateral material. Clockwise from
top right are jeans labels, denim buttons,
a compliments slip and a receipt envelope.*

Acne

** KVITTOKOPIA **

Acne Jeans Retail
Normalmstorg 2
111 46 STOCKHOLM

Telefon: 08-6116411
ORG NR: SE   556642-9683
Kvitto Nr: N35562   Kassa: XE 090420   14:32
Säljare: Fredrik Röhne
~~d:~~ 0200   Butikskassa NT

A-PRIS   SUMMA

Acne Jeans

ACNEARTDEPARTMENT.SE
TEL: +46 8 555 799 00. FAX: +46 8 555 799 99
LILLA NYGATAN 23, BOX 2327, SE-103 18 STOCKHOLM

Referencing each collection, the shopping bag offers another opportunity to reinforce the brand inspirations. Clockwise from top left is 'There are, forever, buildings to be made, music to be composed, art to be created, clothes to be designed and photographs to be taken. But high speed can make for wrong turns, and short cuts can come out in the wrong place. Inspiring are those who break free to find a richer soil, in which to create,' 'Homage to Paul Renner by Acne Jeans 2006.05.03,' 'Homage to Haçienda by Acne 2006.03.24' and the reverse of 'Homage to Paul Renner by Acne Jeans 2006.05.03.'

OPPOSITE : Maximising every opportunity, wrapping tissue paper is customized each season.

MONOLOGUES

Photographs by DANIEL JACKSON

Styling by MATTIAS KARLSSON

NE PAS AFFRANCHIR

NO STAMP REQUIRED

REPLY PAID/REPONSE PAYEE
SWEDEN/SUEDE

ACNE PAPER
SE - 110 05 Stockholm
Sweden

ACNE JEANS PREVIEW, SPRING/SUMMER 07, PHOTO BY ANDREAS LARSSON

WE'RE YOU THINKING OF

ACNE JEANS

Prioritaire
Par Avion

IBRS/CCRI NO: 20 45 42 09

ACNE JEANS

ACNE JEANS

REPLY PAID/REPONSE PAYEE
SWEDEN/SUEDE

ACNE PAPER
SE - 110 05 Stockholm
Sweden

NO STAMP REQUIRED

NE PAS AFFRANCHIR

The refined design aesthetic is carried right
through to the smallest details. Acne Paper
subscription cards get the treatment with
alternating paper colours for each issue.
'We're thinking of you' stamps add a personal
touch to their envelopes while reinforcing the
Acne Jeans mark/button simultaneously.

ANOTHERCOMPANY for
TENUE DE NÎMES

A tentative side project since 2003, Anothercompany was officially launched by Joachim Baan in 2007. The simplicity of the name is an open challenge to look beyond the slick façade of creative agencies, focusing attention on the company's clients and the work it produces for them. While the work is far from anonymous, the emphasis is clearly on the content. There is an aesthetic continuity throughout the visual language that moves between art, fashion, photography and graphic design. "I believe that without pleasure you can't run a proper business. Our business is pleasure, our pleasure is business," says Baan. This commitment and passion is evident in the enormous enthusiasm with which he embraces each project.

Baan is clear about the importance of narrative in his work. "The most important thing in our work is to tell stories." His process starts with thorough research to build an understanding of the client and consumer. The details are then rearranged into original forms, colours and type to compose the new message.

Anothercompany was established in Utrecht before relocating to the creative hub of Amsterdam. Self-educated and highly motivated, Baan is inspired by "simplicity, creativity and detailing". This philosophy is a direct parallel with the label Tenue de Nîmes. An homage to the geographical origin of denim in southern Provence, the historical reference is important in understanding this relatively new brand. "The complete idea was formed around this name. To take something at its very roots and transform it into something new, something now, without losing the heritage." Primarily a boutique, Tenue de Nîmes also offer their own hand-made private label dedicated to high-quality daily wear. Pursuing the modern classic,

Tenue de Nîmes occupy the crossroads between contemporary style and traditional craftsmanship.

Baan worked on the project for ten months prior to its launch at the end of 2008, and has been integral to the development of the company. Although he was initially commissioned as an independent art director, his dedication and engagement with the brand became so vital that he was invited to join Tenue de Nîmes as a partner. This level of appreciation rewards his hard work and acknowledges that his contribution to the brand goes beyond the development of the logo. "I want to work with my clients, rather than for them, to really understand each other and build something together. But it is more important to work in a team with other creatives, to share ideas, sketches, knowledge." Baan has found this with Tenue de Nîmes, and is relishing the exchange of experience and ideas to create something bigger than the sum of the parts.

There is an integrity to raw denim that has been directly translated into the branding. "It is all about history and telling the story in an honest and complete way. In every single aspect of its communication we wanted to implement the concept of denim; a very strong and long-lasting fabric, which evolved into the best and most used basic material in fashion, without losing its 'fashion'. The indigo, the tactility, the quality and the craftsmanship." But more than denim alone, raw materials like cotton, wool and silk form the foundation of Tenue de Nîmes. Clearly inspired by this heritage, Baan created a logo that positions the brand firmly within a modern context.

Baan is not limited to printed matter, and has moved into the retail space to reinforce the brand. Even during construction he took the opportunity to put a stencil of the logo in the window. Aware that any overtly commercial gesture

could alienate Tenue de Nîmes' target audience, who are looking to reinforce their individuality, Baan employs sophisticated details embodied with a personal touch to build a subtle message and atmosphere of consistency for Tenue de Nîmes. For a new brand looking to become established, the authenticity in this approach is extremely valuable in the long term.

The progressive nature of fashion represents a unique challenge and opportunity for Baan. "We find fashion an interesting industry because it is fast, almost fluid and always forward-thinking. More than any other industry it is about creating a perfect world." The aesthetic clarity of Anothercompany is equally aspirational and a perfect match for such requirements.

www.anothercompany.org
www.tenuedenimes.com

While the debut issue N°0 was only available digitally, the success of Journal de Nîmes justified its launch into a quarterly duotone newspaper. With an oversized format of 30 x 42cm (11¼ x 16½in), the publication explores the aesthetic world of Tenue de Nîmes. Like the brand, denim is the primary focus, yet related products and accessories are featured as well. The magazine allows in-depth analysis of the heritage and projected future of denim.

Nº 1.
THE BLUE ISSUE
MAY 2009

THE FIRST PRINTED PAPER FOR
A DENIM INSPIRED BOUTIQUE
WWW.TENUEDENIMES.COM

IN THIS ISSUE:

Journal de Nîmes

Nº 3
THE ONE YEAR
ANNIVERSARY ISSUE
NOVEMBER 2009

THE PRINTED PAPER FOR
A DENIM INSPIRED BOUTIQUE
WWW.TENUEDENIMES.COM

IN THIS ISSUE:

Journal de Nîmes

Nº 2
THE LABOUR ISSUE
SUMMER/AUTUMN 2009

THE PRINTED PAPER FOR
A DENIM INSPIRED BOUTIQUE
WWW.TENUEDENIMES.COM

IN THIS ISSUE:

Relevant to the materiality and hardwearing
qualities of denim, this special heavyweight
cotton bag reinforces the brand values outside
the retail environment. Attention to detail
is shown by the notably shorter handles
to provide more balanced proportions.

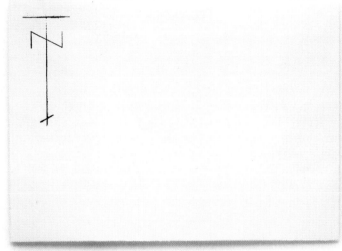

RENE STROLENBERG
RENE@TENUEDENIMES.COM
+31 (0)6 27 299 536

ELANDSGRACHT 60
1016 TX IN AMSTERDAM
THE NETHERLANDS

MENNO VAN MEURS
MENNO@TENUEDENIMES.COM
+31 (0)6 484 30 392

A DENIM INSPIRED BOUTIQUE

INFO@TENUEDENIMES.COM
WWW.TENUEDENIMES.COM
+31 (0)20 320 40 12

ELANDSGRACHT 60
1016 TX IN AMSTERDAM
THE NETHERLANDS

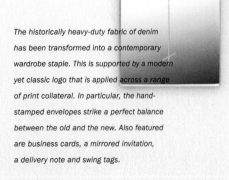

The historically heavy-duty fabric of denim
has been transformed into a contemporary
wardrobe staple. This is supported by a modern
yet classic logo that is applied across a range
of print collateral. In particular, the hand-
stamped envelopes strike a perfect balance
between the old and the new. Also featured
are business cards, a mirrored invitation,
a delivery note and swing tags.

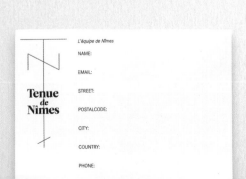

L'équipe de Nîmes

NAME:

EMAIL:

STREET:

POSTALCODE:

CITY:

COUNTRY:

PHONE:

BUERO NEW YORK for KAI KÜHNE

Buero New York is one of a small handful of leading creative agencies that specialize in the fashion, beauty and lifestyle industries. Led by Alex Wiederin, a charismatic yet modest Austrian, it has earned a global reputation for insightful image creation supported by distinct, innovative font design. Determined to establish an independent studio as a progression from his first company, Buero X, which was based in Vienna, Wiederin had the confidence to launch Buero New York in the aftermath of the 11 September 2001 attacks on the World Trade Center. In recent years this boutique studio has evolved into a think-tank for luxury brands, and for creative minds as they collectively discover and define future trends. It does not have a specific look yet has developed a trademark presence through the creative direction of a vast range of contemporary fashion and lifestyle magazines. More than graphic design or creativity, communication lies at the heart of this process.

Because of its seasonal reinvention and overall visual emphasis, the fashion industry has an immediate appeal for people who are creatively adventurous. "You need to have the interest in your product in order to design something good. You need to understand it," says Wiederin. For this reason he is careful to analyze and produce work for the end consumer, not only for the client. This is fundamental to the way Buero approach every project.

While the studio is best known for working on global fashion brands, it also supports emerging talent. Kai Kühne launched his label in Spring/Summer 2006 and Buero have continued to manage all areas of its visual communication. Known for his complex patterns and eccentric style, Kühne is a flamboyant member of the New York fashion scene, who attracts attention in equal measure both on and off the catwalk. Wiederin found a graphic solution that would represent the designer's personality and allow it to grow in different directions. Kühne's signature became the central motif of the branding: it represents, "the graphicness of his shapes, and his spirit to swim against the stream". An equally fluid typographic treatment is used for supporting information that projects a sense of individuality. Because there are none of the sometimes restrictive obligations of quantity associated with more established brands, Buero can explore bespoke and intricate solutions for the label. Production techniques such as multilayered folds and foil blocking have become as much a part of the brand communication as the typography. This flexibility is immediately identifiable with the vibrancy of the Kai Kühne line.

"It is a close collaboration," says Wiederin. "I learn from the people around me, so the collaboration between the people I work with and my clients is the most essential thing for me to create." This sentiment is compounded by the professional relationships that over the years have developed into friendships. Through constant dialogue Wiederin avoids having to be stubborn or forceful, the priority is to ensure that ideas and inspiration continue to flow. It becomes clear that the fast pace of fashion requires all participants to function collectively to avoid stagnation and delays.

The ability to nurture the natural talents of others is central to Wiederin's role as a problem solver. Confidence in his clients and collaborators allows him to focus on the bigger picture. The obvious pleasure he receives from his profession is contagious, yet he maintains constant clarity about the task at hand: "We are here to make communication. Design must function." Surrounded by the insatiable creative demands and distractions of fashion, this practicality is irreplaceable.

www.buero-newyork.com
www.kaikuhne.com

"I think what's unique about the identity is the way we use type." Inspired by the signature of Kai Kühne there is a distinct fluidity to the typographic treatment throughout the brand communication. The flexibility of the composition shown in the business card, envelope and compliments slip feels cohesive and progressive. The Autumn/Winter 2006/07 invitation also refers to the structural quality of the collection.

DEEVA-HA for GAR—DE

With a casual collaboration stretching back to their college days, Pete Deevakul and Jiminie Ha worked together occasionally for three years before they officially launched DEEVA-HA in 2010. Their backgrounds are in photography and graphic design respectively, and they have merged these complementary yet independent disciplines with their creative process and raw creative energy. Based in New York, they are inspired by their immediate surroundings. "We work using materials and equipment that are at hand. We take advantage of our limitations and turn them into points of departure," says Ha. This proactive attitude infuses their work with a spontaneous energy that is particularly attractive to the fashion industry.

GAR—DE is a collective that has been an ongoing project for Deevakul and Ha since they were commissioned to establish the branding for its debut Autumn/Winter 2008/09 collection. Mutual enthusiasm ensured that the relationship, initially based on the conventional designer/client model, became a close collaboration. Deevakul and Ha were encouraged to take creative ownership of the project and thrived with the added responsibility. "The only restriction was the budget, which never really affected our creative process," says Ha. "We took this as a challenge to make the images more intriguing and tell a story that went beyond the clothing line. In fact, it's those constraints that have allowed us to find new ways to present the GAR—DE line season after season. We have the freedom to interpret the brand in a unique way that simultaneously respects and subverts traditional means in fashion."

Its name derived from the French for 'to guard', GAR—DE explore the constant challenges to personal boundaries presented by today's congested and fast-paced society. Its first collection featured highly durable leather outerwear to establish an authentic aesthetic for the brand that went beyond seasonal trends. With longevity as the line's central focus, GAR—DE's response to fashion's cyclical nature is subtle updates and steady expansion rather than continual reinvention of the same garments.

Ha developed a close bond with GAR—DE while working on the first collection, and its three founding members – Christopher Viggiano, Jonathan Delagarde and Ken Li – invited her to join the collective. Ha was initially primarily responsible for visual branding but has become involved across all areas of the business. Completely integrated into the dialogue of the brand, she contributes throughout the process. Given the flexible structure of the collective, she needs to adapt to the creative input of others while maintaining the clarity of the visual message. "We like to think of what we do as being rich with the energy of youthful fashion, tempered by a cleverness and sophistication born out of necessity."

DEEVA-HA have transferred their self-awareness into the branding of GAR—DE. "We intend to make every project an extension of our own process as artists and professionals in the commercial world." There is also a sense of humour, as they challenge preconceived notions about fashion. The rubber-stamp letterhead subverts the industry's conventional perfection and offers an accessible alternative that feels fresh and immediate. This conceptual tension builds a complexity in the message of the brand as it evolves each season.

Intent on breaking away from the computer, DEEVA-HA develop concepts and strategies that combine the hand-made with the machine. They have found the balance between photography and graphic design, their creative process seems effortless as they operate with a freedom that is not restricted by any discipline. DEEVA-HA and GAR—DE are a perfect example of how a collaborative professional relationship can become greater than its individual parts. "It's all about making something significant out of absolutely nothing."

Letterheads feature a hand-stamped logo with varying degrees of legibility, reaffirming the unconventional aesthetic of GAR—DE. Additional information is printed at the top and bottom of the page further distancing the material from standard expectations.

"For every fantastic idea we have about representing the line, the thought of utility brings about another dimension. And given the constraints, we often find ourselves looking at what is readily available and re-imagining it to fit our needs." The selection of lookbooks adopt a unique format each season that best suits the collection.

135 West 36th St. 5th Fl.
New York NY 10018

T: 212.967.8826
F: 212.695.5328

Jonathan Delagarde

john@gar-de.com
T: 347.405.2196

GAR——DE

135 West 36th St.
6th Fl.
New York NY 10018

T +1 212.967.8826
F +1 212.947.6130

Jen Kim

www.gar-de.com
jen@gar-de.com

GAR——DE

135 West 36th St. 5th Fl.
New York NY 10018

T: 212.967.8826
F: 212.695.5328

Ken Li

ken@gar-de.com
T: 917.371.8977

GAR——DE

Each business card features the logo in a slightly different position. The dash stretches to the back of the card, reinforcing the three-dimensionality of the object.

MEVIS AND VAN DEURSEN for
VIKTOR & ROLF

Since starting their Amsterdam-based studio in 1987, Armand Mevis and Linda van Deursen have refined their vision of graphic design to see it as an active part of the message rather than simply a vehicle for communication. Recipients of much critical acclaim, they have become prominent figures in the progression of the discipline. As educators, and in conjunction with their practice, they have been able to impart their energy and integrity to a new generation of designers to the benefit of the wider profession.

Working predominantly for public sector and cultural institutions, Mevis and van Deursen are pleasantly surprised by the success of their relationship with Viktor & Rolf and the personal satisfaction it brings. It was a commission from the Stedelijk Museum of Modern Art in 1997 to design an invitation for a Viktor & Rolf exhibition that first brought them together. Viktor & Rolf have always occupied a unique, almost interchangeable, area between fashion and art. The commission gave Mevis and van Deursen a stepping stone into the world of fashion when they became responsible for the invitations to the first Viktor & Rolf haute couture show in Paris. Constrained by an impossibly short deadline, minimal funding and a lack of brand identity, the invitations were "none of the things that we intended to make and maybe not exactly what they had wanted, but they functioned well," admits van Deursen.

Due to the bespoke nature of haute couture there was little need to establish a formalized logo for Viktor & Rolf. It was not until the launch of the prêt-à-porter line for Autumn/Winter 2000/01 that a distinction between the company's collections was required. Rather than dictate a complete branding system, Mevis and van Deursen opened their dialogue with a range of elements, allowing Viktor & Rolf to experiment with them. "They had a clear idea of where they wanted to be and how they wanted their fashion to be received. And that was quite in the league of the big fashion houses in Paris." Viktor & Rolf were always aware of the need to appear established; it was a game and Mevis and van Deursen were happy to play along.

With a background in Dutch modernism, Mevis and van Deursen had confidence in the aesthetic tradition of their previous commissions. Viktor & Rolf were in pursuit of a fashion language dominated by an unfamiliar French heritage. "Fashion (and the language of fashion) works on a subconscious level. It appeals to the subconscious and because of that we probably (also subconsciously) made a connection with the surrealists, who tried to liberate the imagination through hypnosis, dream analysis and so on," says van Deursen. Mevis and van Deursen were drawn to Salvador Dalí's soft watch as inspiration for the seal. While old-fashioned, the seal was without any real function and slightly out of proportion, and when used in black it produced "a posh, absurd, fetish-like quality that suited Viktor & Rolf. It is something you cannot really say why, but all those elements together really worked for them."

Viktor & Rolf were so enthusiastic about the logo that before it was finished they started applying it to their garments in all sorts of materials, colours and finishes. This period of experimentation lasted for approximately two seasons before they commissioned a full suite of print collateral that fixed the parameters for the brand into the refined message it is today. During this exercise, Mevis and van Deursen were able to draw on the extensive practical research involved in designing the print material.

Up until then there was very little funding in Viktor & Rolf's career but the end result had to look expensive. The prohibitive set-up costs of foil stamping and embossing for a range of sizes, from letterheads to swing tags, resulted in the use of a single-sized logo for all formats. Financial restrictions actually built greater consistency and relevance into how the seal was used.

Viktor & Rolf exercise a conceptual economy that results in a unique clarity. "Their ideas are so direct you can summarize them in one line," says van Deursen. With such precision, little explanation is required for Mevis and van Deursen to proceed with the invitations to the seasonal collections. While Viktor & Rolf are sometimes able to translate the concept of a collection into a viable print format, there is no obligation for Mevis and van Deursen to follow their direction exclusively. "We do not deny our qualities or interests, we really try to make something we like that also works for them." In what is not a collaboration in the truest sense, Mevis and van Deursen are bound to the concept of the collection while Viktor & Rolf independently explore applications for the logo. This mutual trust has allowed the brand to maintain a freshness throughout the years.

While Mevis and van Deursen originally treated the invitations and lookbooks from each collection as individual creative challenges, they have now developed a framework that allows greater refinement and efficiency. "There is always a unique character to each collection that it is possible to line the invitations to." Invitations are always presented on letterhead paper and the lookbooks utilize an A5 format with complementary black and white covers for menswear and womenswear respectively. This foundation allows greater conceptual exploration and clarity, and also supports the impression of an established fashion house.

The Viktor & Rolf brand expanded dramatically, and while success resulted in more careful time management, their relationship with Mevis and van Deursen has remained constant. Hindsight has validated their initial instinct in shaping the brand. "I think it was a unique and funny situation how the branding has arrived," says van Deursen. "If they were not able to express their strong ideas so clearly we would never have known how to work for them."

There is a natural confidence in the way Mevis and van Deursen rationalize their process that disguises the complexity of their practice. While their output is an exercise in precision, there is a duality in the fact that they are comfortable with allowing events to unfold. The commercial component of Viktor & Rolf immediately sets them apart from their other clients, yet this unfamiliarity has enhanced Mevis and van Deursen's satisfaction. "It started quite innocently but Viktor & Rolf also became the most successful and well-known client we have."

www.mevisvandeursen.nl
www.viktor-rolf.com

VIKTOR & ROLF

WITH COMPLIMENTS

HOBBEMASTRAAT 12 / NL–1071 ZB AMSTERDAM
OFFICE@VIKTOR-ROLF.COM / WWW.VIKTOR-ROLF.COM
T +31(0)20 419 6188 / F +31(0)20 330 6221

VIKTOR & ROLF

PRINS HENDRIKKADE 100 / NL–1011 AH AMSTERDAM
OFFICE@VIKTOR-ROLF.COM
T +31(0)20 419 6188 / F +31(0)20 330 6221

Originally the logo was used at the same size
on all print communication to minimize costs,
but the visual consistency has become a
strength of the brand. "We designed something
for them that was a little innocent, but we had
a clear goal and ambition from Viktor & Rolf,
to try and make something that would work
for them to achieve their ambitions, it was
more like playing a game and when it finally
became really serious it did work."

VIKTOR & ROLF
HOBBEMASTRAAT 12 / NL–1071 ZB AMSTERDAM
OFFICE@VIKTOR-ROLF.COM / WWW.VIKTOR-ROLF.COM
T +31(0)20 419 6188 / F +31(0)20 330 6221
ABN AMRO BANK / DAM 2 / AMSTERDAM / THE NETHERLANDS
ACC NR 56.57.20.023 VIKTOR & ROLF B.V. / SWIFTCODE ABN ANL 2A
VAT NL 80 84 75 526 B 01

Viktor & Rolf invite you to attend
the Fall / Winter 2002/2003 show
Saturday March 9 at 18:30 H
at Studio Gabriel
9, Avenue Gabriel - 75008 Paris

*Long live
the immaterial !*

HR/ROLF
REAU SYLVIE DRUMBACH T 01 42339316 / F 01 40264353
PR CONSULTING   T 212 2288101 / F 212 2288787

VIKTOR & ROLF
INVITE YOU TO ATTEND
THE FW 06|07 SHOW
MONDAY FEBRUARY 27
AT 3.30 PM

ESPACE EPHEMERE -
JARDIN DES TUILERIES
GRAND BASSIN DE
LA CONCORDE, ENTREE
GRILLE D'HONNEUR
CONCORDE
PARIS 1ER

PRESS EU KARLA OTTO   TEL 003314261455 FAX 0033142405903
PRESS US PR CONSULTING   TEL 0012122393901 FAX 0012122393787

VIKTOR & ROLF
INVITE YOU TO ATTEND THE
AUTUMN/WINTER 2009 FASHION SHOW
MONDAY, MARCH 9TH 2009 - 4:30 PM
ESPACE EPHÉMÈRE FREYSSINET
55, BOULEVARD VINCENT AURIOL
75013 PARIS

RSVP

PRESS: KARLA OTTO +33 1 48 61 34 36
SALES: STAFF INTERNATIONAL +33 1 48 00 08 69

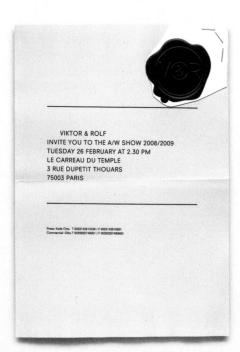

VIKTOR & ROLF
INVITE YOU TO THE A/W SHOW 2008/2009
TUESDAY 26 FEBRUARY AT 2.30 PM
LE CARREAU DU TEMPLE
3 RUE DUPETIT THOUARS
75003 PARIS

Press: Karla Otto   T 0033142613436 / F 0033142615891
Commercial: Gibo   T 0039025748061 / F 0039025748060

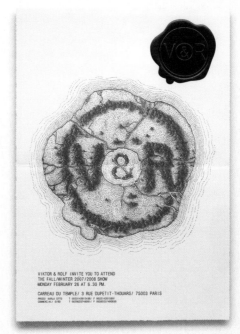

VIKTOR & ROLF INVITE YOU TO ATTEND
THE FALL/WINTER 2007/2008 SHOW
MONDAY FEBRUARY 26 AT 6.30 PM

CARREAU DU TEMPLE/ 3 RUE DUPETIT-THOUARS/ 75003 PARIS
PRESS: KARLA OTTO   T 0033142613436/ F 0033142615891
COMMERCIAL: GIBO   T 0039025748061/ F 0039025748060

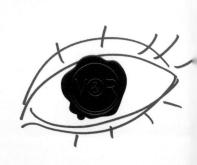

S/S SHOW 2008, TUESDAY OCTOBER 2ND AT 2.30 PM
ESPACE ÉPHÉMÈRE DES TUILERIES, CARRÉ DES SANGLIERS
ACCÈS: GRILLE D'HONNEUR, PLACE DE LA CONCORDE
PRESS/ KARLA OTTO   T 0033142613436/ F 0033142615891
COMMERCIAL/ GIBO   T 0039025748061/ F 0039025748060

38

invite you to attend the Spring Summer 2005 Show
Wednesday, October 6th at 4.30 pm

Espace Ephemere - Jardin des Tuileries
Grand Bassin de la Concorde
Entrée Grille d'Honneur Concorde
Paris 1er

*All invitations are based on the standard
letterhead format. Working within this
restricted framework Mevis and van Deursen
are able to creatively explore a wide range
of conceptual iterations that directly reflect
the upcoming collection. "If we put the seal
in a different colour, then I always think we
should not have done that, it should not
have been red, it should not have been gold.
Maybe there are some exceptions but usually
I only like it when it is black."*

For the Spring/Summer 2003 collection every invitation was an original hand-made design by students of Mevis and van Deursen. As original objects they immediately transformed the conventional letterhead paper into a covetable object. "There is always a clear departing point that gives the collection a unique character and it is always possible to look at the invitations and link them back to the collections."

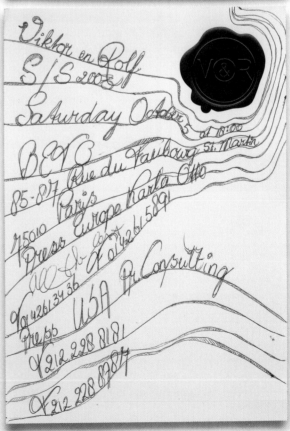

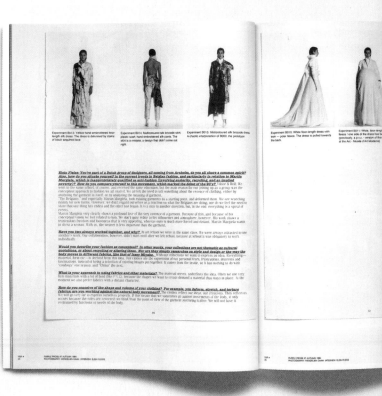

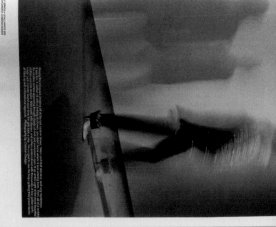

Published in 2003 to celebrate ten years of Viktor & Rolf, the ABCDE Magazine subverts the medium with an innovative branding exercise presenting an edited selection of their press clippings. The end result feels like a normal magazine. To complete the effect advertisements from other brands were also featured. "Viktor & Rolf always have fantastic ideas to begin with. They have a super simple strategy that is always a good basis to start from as a designer, it is almost as if you only have to do half the work."

Branding MEVIS AND VAN DEURSEN for VIKTOR & ROLF

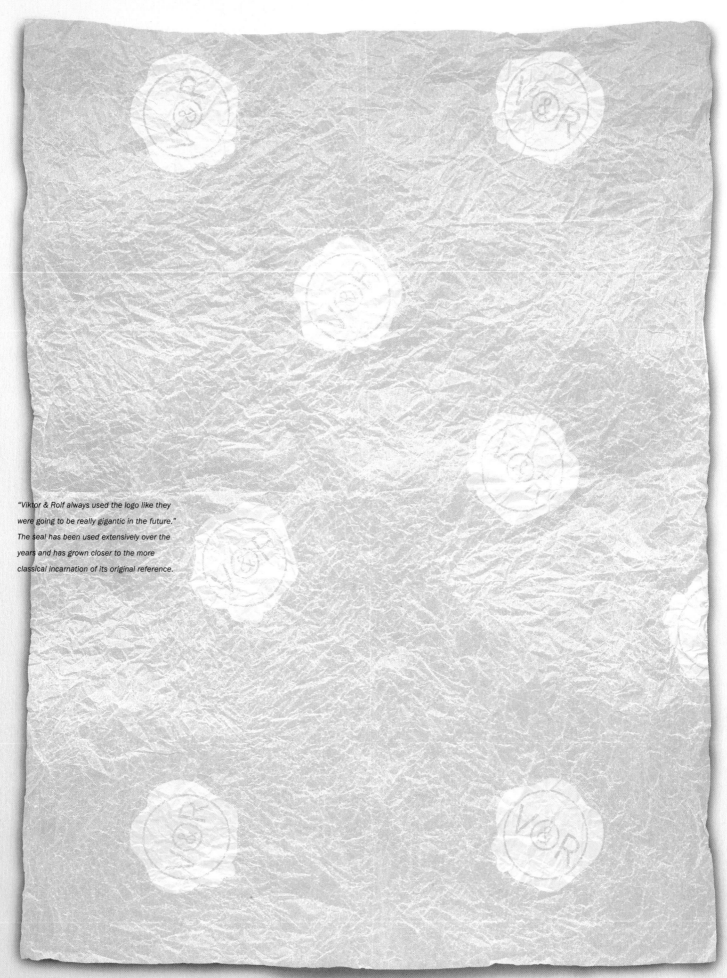

"Viktor & Rolf always used the logo like they
were going to be really gigantic in the future."
The seal has been used extensively over the
years and has grown closer to the more
classical incarnation of its original reference.

S/S 2005

S/S 2005   VIKTOR®ROLF

01   MARLEEN
COAT   VDJ500A VJ116 790

03
COAT

S/S 2005   VIKTOR®ROLF

S/S 2005

"To always print invitations on their stationery, to use the same size and same elements, I thought I would be really happy to do something similar with the lookbooks as well." Working with the industry standard of catwalk photography, Mevis and van Deursen create a subtle integration between the men's and women's collections. The two covers act as counterweights, the women's collection has a white cover with images only printed on the left-hand page and vice versa for the men's collection. The logos on the cover are standard size too. A literal inversion of each other, together they represent a conceptual whole. "We do not have to convince them of our ideas every time, it is quite the opposite. We know exactly what they want and we make fast decisions."

Branding MEVIS AND VAN DEURSEN for VIKTOR & ROLF

S/S 2009

790
210
730

03

JACKET	VUS005A	VS002	790
KNIT	VUS607R	VS900	010
TROUSERS	VUS202A	VS002	790

S/S 2009   VIKTOR & ROLF

Branding MEVIS AND VAN DEURSEN for VIKTOR & ROLF

MORE STUDIO for ZUCZUG /

MORE Studio exhibit a distinctive, raw aesthetic in their work. They reinterpret conventional structures and employ conceptual twists that expose the integrity of their process. With a focus on typography, the message is immediate yet offers layered complexity and depth. Central to MORE's practice is defining and balancing the unique requirements of each client with the demands of the audience: "We spend more time on research and communication than design." The Shanghai-based studio started in 2006 and are dedicated to achieving a sense of timelessness in their designs.

For MORE, every client provides a unique opportunity, and they are fascinated by the creative potential of the fashion industry. Graphic design is often focused on visual beauty, which easily translates into an appreciation of fashion. "The fashion industry is a very important part of people's daily lives. Clothes, food, lodging and transportation are all subtly influenced by fashion. Some fashion has a very strong visual symbol; it can even affect people's values and behaviour as consumers. Fashion influences graphic design, and it is influenced by graphic design also."

Although China has always been a source of inspiration for designers and artists, it is relatively new on the international fashion scene. ZUCZUG / were established in 2002, by Wang Yiyang, and are focused on pioneering a unique, contemporary Chinese fashion language. They are also based in Shanghai, a chance meeting with MORE resulted in the studio being commissioned to design their website. A close relationship immediately developed and MORE were entrusted with the complete branding programme for the label. "In addition to garments and products we want ZUCZUG / to represent a new lifestyle and attitude."

Fashion offers MORE a unique set of branding requirements. "Our challenge is to build a special visual language that is simple, direct, effective and identifiable. Originality is also very important." Beyond developing a conventional mark, the studio has redefined the basic function of the logo: the simple act of adding a forward slash at its end transforms it from static object into the building block of the brand. The impression that more information is available is a powerful message and builds consistency. A loose reference to the URL naming structure, the concept is immediately identifiable and flexible. Its success has seen the logo incorporated in every level of the brand, from garments to business cards.

While MORE are entrusted with the seasonal reinvention of the fashion label's visual communication, they have respect and admiration for Wang and depend on his input. "Collaboration is an effective way to work, drawing on the strength of both sides. ZUCZUG / give us enough time and once we have a suitable idea anything is possible." Constant dialogue and collective refinement ensure the best results. MORE believe the creative background they share with their client is an important factor in achieving this level of collaboration. While the skills of both parties differ, the natural respect that arises from their similar mindsets creates an intuitive understanding.

"Design can communicate with mind, sense and emotion. It has unlimited possibilities and challenges." MORE are enthusiastic about their role as designers and become personally involved in their projects. They are undistracted by trends, and strip back the visual elements of their work to focus on conceptual exploration and structural innovation. MORE are a relatively new company but are clearly at the forefront of China's growing creative industry.

www.itismore.cn
www.zuczug.com

ZUCZUG / 0

The structure and potential for expansion of
the naming convention is particularly evident
when applied to the garment labels.

ZUCZUG/4/165/84A

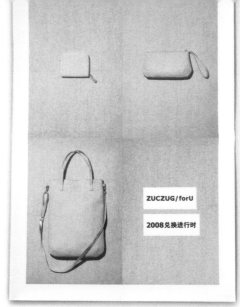

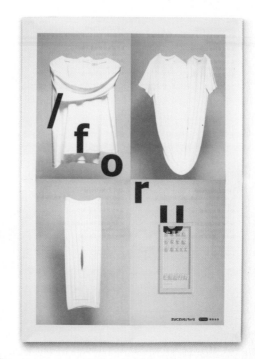

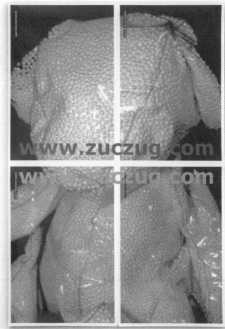

The retail environment of ZUCZUG / is refreshed monthly with large A0 posters with identifiable quadrant perforations. "Usually the posters are images of models wearing the current collection. Sometimes we make special designs to promote the launch of a new product range."

Branding MORE STUDIO for ZUCZUG /

The strength of the naming convention is particularly important in defining the wide range of diffusion lines. While most print collateral – like the business cards and compliments slips – use the main logo, the swing tags obviously cover the full range. The hand symbol signifies the basic range; a more sporty collection is identified by the 'O,' special VIP gifts are under 'forU'; 'blue' indicates the denim line.

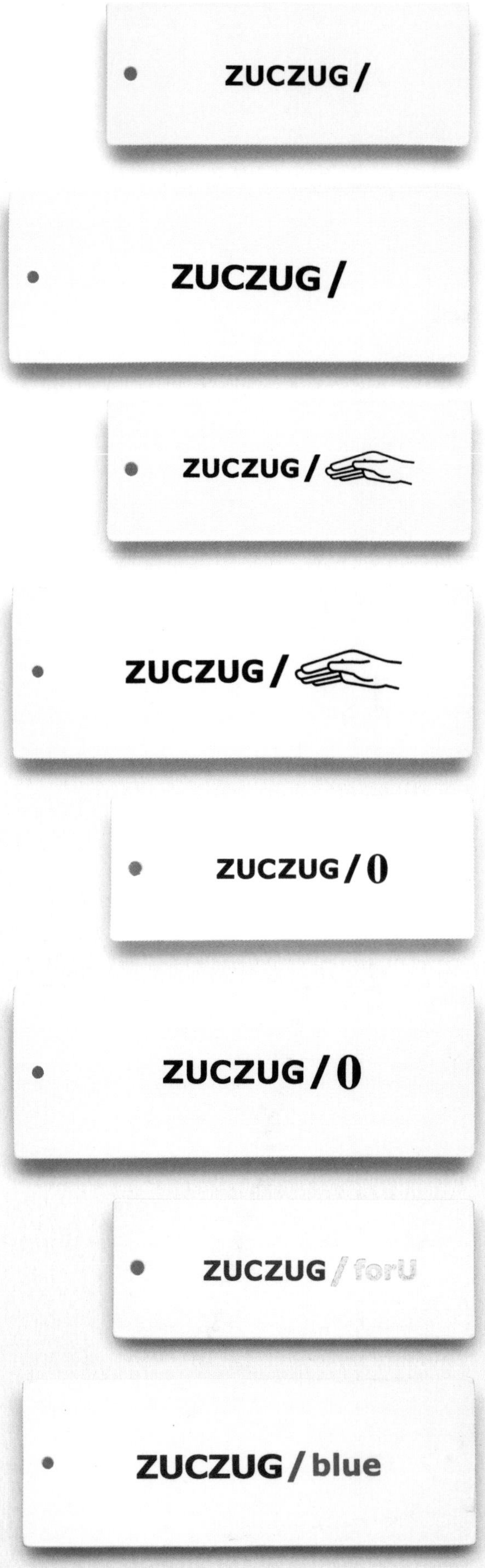

ZUCZUG /

ZUCZUG /

ZUCZUG /

ZUCZUG /

ZUCZUG / 0

ZUCZUG / 0

ZUCZUG / forU

ZUCZUG / blue

ZUCZUG / 江晓舟 / 品牌管理部
视觉陈列 / Jiang Xiaozhou
Brand Department
Visual Merchandising

ZUCZUG /

ZUCZUG / 上海素然服饰有限公司 / 上海市昭化路357号C幢5楼 / www.zuczug.com
Shanghai Suran Fashion Co., LTD. / 5F, No.357, Bldg C, Zhaohua Rd., Shanghai, 200050 /
Tel: 8621-6252 9763 / 6252 9765 /
Fax: 8621-6252 1785

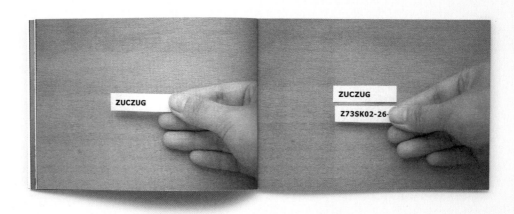

On the launch of the branding exercise
a book was produced to clearly explain
the logic behind the new treatment to
all managers in their retail stores. Due to the
clarity of the branding little written explanation
was necessary as MORE highlighted practical
examples through photographic comparison.

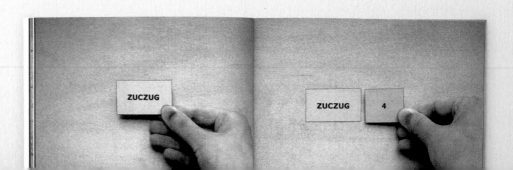

请登陆
www.zuczug.com

To promote the launch of the new website in 2006 an A3 poster with a recreation of the ZUCZUG / homepage was available in all stores.

OHLSONSMITH for VAN DEURS

In addition to the conventional battle over form and function, Ohlsonsmith are committed to the emotional impact of their practice. They pay particular attention to the 'feel' of their work and their ultimate goal is to produce a memorable experience. Based in Stockholm, the studio was founded in 2006 by Barbro Ohlson Smith. With expertise in print, motion and experience design, the studio's strength lies in brand identity development. Ohlsonsmith understand the marketplace is fiercely competitive and believe innovative design is a vital means of building value, strength and, most importantly, distinction from the competition for their clients.

Having previously met the designer of van Deurs, Susanne Beskow, on several occasions, Ohlson Smith saw one of her early fashion presentations and was immediately drawn to the collection. However, there was a clear disparity between the luxurious quality of the garments and the brand's mediocre visual communication. Convinced of its potential, and excited by the opportunity to work on a project that interested her personally, Ohlson Smith offered her services. The priority was to reflect the high quality of the garments across every level of the experience. Instead of design concepts, the first presentation to van Deurs was a moodboard of images, textiles and textures that defined the brand and clarified how it should be perceived. This visual gesture had an immediate, positive impact: Ohlsonsmith had clearly demonstrated their understanding of the van Deurs brand and earned the company's trust.

Van Deurs is a relatively small label, a fact that affords Ohlsonsmith the opportunity to manage the entire brand. Ohlson Smith happily admits, "We seem to want to get involved everywhere. When we have the chance

In an industry dominated by boutique labels, Ohlsonsmith provide an invaluable service by establishing an identifiable brand image. "Fashion offers the possibility to create new expressions without any connection to the real world. Because of this, the possibilities are endless and the artistic freedom vast." In a true balance between the heart and mind, Ohlsonsmith have been able to give clarity of form to the key values of van Deurs and drive the brand forward with confidence.

to influence the entire brand, we get great satisfaction from that. We have a very good understanding and respect for each other. Susanne has put a lot of trust in us." The personal engagement with Beskow instils an emotional weight in the final product that is not possible with larger labels. This intimacy is reflected by the passion Ohlsonsmith bring to the project.

With an emphasis on the tactility of the fabric, the van Deurs signature is pleated garments, and this has been adopted as the central element of the branding. "When you see the pleated material a lot of thoughts come at you straightaway. The swing tag was one of the ideas we had quite early." A moment of inspiration arrived with the delivery of a parcel of fabric neatly wrapped in pleated paper. This was immediately adapted as a package for a press kit. In a continual extension on the theme, simulated creases and angular lines of type were used in the Autumn/Winter 2007/08 lookbook to reinforce this tactile quality. Ohlsonsmith have cleverly realigned the focus of the brand from the form of the logo to the actual touch and feel of the product.

An open dialogue between Ohlsonsmith and van Deurs is vital to stimulate new ideas. Despite a close professional bond, there is a separation of responsibilities rather than full collaboration. Ohlsonsmith are decisive about how the brand should be presented. "We provide an extra dimension to extend the core message of van Deurs and allow Susanne to focus on what she does best," says Ohlson Smith. In a reversal of conventional roles, Ohlsonsmith take the initiative, making creative proposals to Beskow. More than brand designers, they are brand guardians, and even advise on marketing and business issues to consolidate and focus the message.

www.ohlsonsmith.se
www.vandeurs.se

The simplicity of the pleated swing tag, designed by Petter Hollström and Barbro Ohlson Smith, is central to the brand communication of van Deurs . "A proud logotype for a proud brand."

The Autumn/Winter 2007/08 lookbook, with
photography by Knotan, emphasized black
as the central theme from the collection.
Printed on uncoated paper it appears to
absorb the images directly into the texture
of the paper. Postcards are also used
as seasonal promotional material.

Branding OHLSONSMITH for VAN DEURS

Seizing the raw packaging material of the pleated fabric from the van Deurs studio, Ohlsonsmith developed an envelope for an early press release. Here the tactility of pleated material is immediately apparent.

SANDERSON BOB for YUTAKA TAJIMA

While building a reputation as a prolific talent at leading design studios, Bob Sanderson produced an increasing range of independent creative projects until they began to demand his full attention. It was then a natural progression to establish his eponymous studio in 2004. His infectious enthusiasm for creativity translates into the use of visually arresting, high-impact graphics and colour. Sanderson embraces the collective strength of collaboration and has built an extensive network of creatives through Yutaka Tajima.

One year prior to starting his studio, Sanderson launched Yutaka Tajima, a side project and his pursuit of more creative freedom. More than a T-shirt label, it was intended to initiate collaboration with a vast range of people. "To create something free from preconceived ideas," says Sanderson. Having developed a simple geometric 'Y' logo, the brand undergoes continual and wholesale change as contributors are invited to interpret the basic mark. Sanderson is eager to receive visual, conceptual or even mathematical translations of the form, the project is a true blank canvas. "We make T-shirts with one colour ink and one logo. It just depends on what people turn it into. That is the simple parameters of it." From this common starting point the options are endless. Initially a casual exercise predominately supported by close friends, through the open submission process Yutaka Tajima has expanded organically and remains self-sufficient.

As a fashion label Yutaka Tajima is a literal branding exercise, shifting the focus and creativity from the product solely onto the logo. While conventional logos tend to shout their allegiance, the abstraction of this message lends to a more subtle approach. It is an open concept, free from structure and restrictions, a fluctuating idea for everyone to interpret in their own way.

"Some people have made the logo into a character while others have absolutely obliterated it until quite unrecognizable. We believe this variation actually strengthens the original brand." Due to the dependence on contributions there is an implied collective ownership of Yutaka Tajima. Profits are shared with the original logo designer, reinforcing the project as a vehicle of creative expression rather than commercial gain. Without financial obligations there is no pressure to generate sales, allowing the focus to remain on creative exploration.

More than a single logo, Sanderson is building a visual archive of the brand. "When you get to 50 or 60 and you can see the different variations, the parameters really change. With increased volume, the depth of the ideas is really endless." To this effect, repetition of ideas is actually a positive way of revealing similarities and sub-categories. Sanderson intends to document the process with a series of books and actually considers this the ultimate goal of the project. Only when considered as a collective whole will these publications reveal the true value of the exercise.

The usual concerns of shifting social trends or brand stagnation are completely irrelevant; longevity will only add further complexity and innovation to the message. In contrast to general practice, Yutaka Tajima is in a constant state of invention, resisting all form of creative control. Rather than graphic designer or fashion designer, Sanderson functions as a facilitator. By subverting conventional branding practice, Sanderson has inadvertently built a tremendously solid and progressive brand with loyal supporters. The result offers insight into commercial brand evolution and innovation where the logo contributes to the message rather than simply function as the anchor.

www.sandersonbob.com
www.yutakatajima.com

The true beauty of the Yutaka Tajima branding is its variability. The larger central logo represents the original form that has been repeatedly interpreted. The basic instructions are: 1 Colour – Pantone Solid 289. The 'Y' can be an integral part or a small detail of the overall design. Final artwork can be 300dpi or vector-based. Designers from left to right, top to bottom: Jethro Haynes, Alexander Bettler, Julian Morey, Jethro Haynes, Carl Burgess, James Goggin, HORT, Bygg Studio, original logo by Sanderson Bob, Chris Bolton, Nicola Pecoraro, Will Bryant, Lars Morell, David Rule, Ian Lyman, Jethro Haynes, Eric Ellis, Maxim Zhestkov, Henrik Nygren Design.

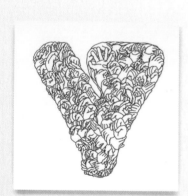

STILETTO NYC for threeASFOUR

Stiletto operate around a work philosophy of "quality, surprise and experimentation" say founding partners Stefanie Barth and Julie Hirschfeld. They have had great success translating their creativity into a broad range of applications, from motion to print, commercial to more experimental. When approaching a new project, they identify the most obvious solutions and immediately cast them aside. This begins to function like 'creative stepping stones', allowing their ideas to move as fast as possible to an unexpected point in the distance. The results are identifiable within the conventions of form and function, yet on closer inspection are conceptually embellished with abstract 'twists'. The creative liberties that they take are justified by the clear conceptual nature of their projects.

In the creative melting pot of Lower East Side Manhattan, the neighbouring studios and shared ambition of Stiletto and what was then asFOUR provided the foundation of the relationship. From a simple commission to design an invitation in 2004, mutual appreciation quickly developed into today's solid partnership. "It's very nice that they respect our work as much as we do theirs," says Barth. "That's what keeps the relationship interesting."

While there is a certain advantage to working with a single creative director, asFOUR work as a collective of four. What might be considered a precarious situation for Stiletto actually provides a framework for open discussion. "I believe many fashion designers have an idea of what they want to represent, so collaboration seems to be more common," says Barth. Encouraged by asFOUR to explore the forms of Arabic script, Stiletto integrated and abstracted the key letterforms into a distinct, unified mark. Supplementary typography is minimal and functional to not distract from the logo.

In 2005 asFOUR split acrimoniously, with one member leaving the collective. Because of the implications for the brand name, Stiletto were asked to rebrand the remaining members into threeASFOUR. "The idea was to keep continuity – apart from the logo, the identity was not changed," says Barth. Skilfully and succinctly, Stiletto navigated this challenge by nestling a '3' beside the original mark. While maintaining visual consistency, they were able to enhance the overall form. The result is more than an improvement, it feels like it was always meant to be.

Being the creators of the original identity grants Stiletto greater freedom to develop the brand's potential further. From dramatic variation in scale to cropping the edges of the mark, they continue to progress the visual presence of threeASFOUR, a vital requirement in the seasonal fashion industry. "We try to understand how they like to be seen and then we create a graphic language/vocabulary to express it," says Barth. Maintaining focus on the end product, 'construction, experimental and modular' are recurring keywords for threeASFOUR and can be seen throughout Stiletto's work.

Stiletto do not subscribe to the perceived advantages of working with a creative client; they put more stock in "personality, vision and articulation". Well equipped with an internal structure of collaboration, threeASFOUR are able to inspire a collective dialogue about their work. In this environment of mutual respect the process continually evolves to suit each project individually. Immediate approval of the design concept is not a measure of success as further revisions add complexity to the end product. Both Stiletto and threeASFOUR appreciate that if all the diverse members involved can be satisfied, the end result will have broad appeal.

www.stilettonyc.com
www.threeasfour.com

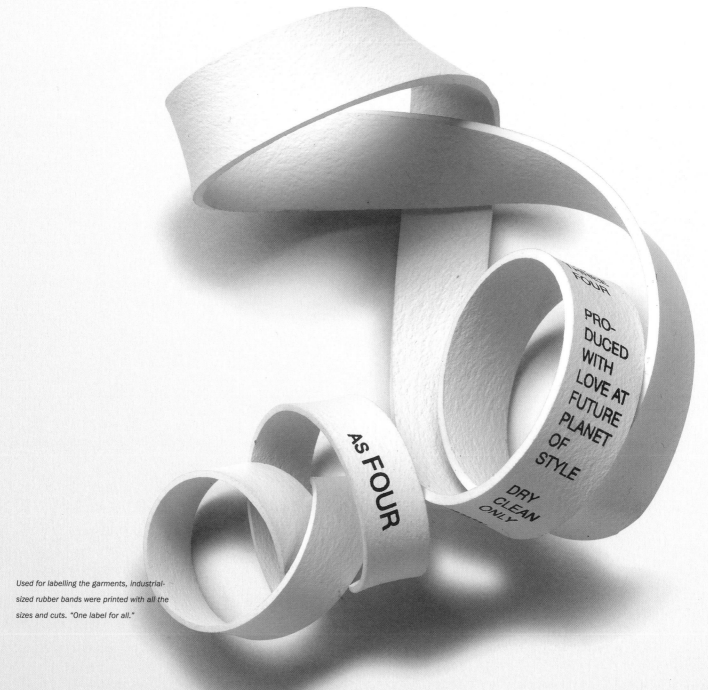

THREE
FOUR

PRO-
DUCED
WITH
LOVE AT
FUTURE
PLANET
OF
STYLE

DRY
CLEAN
ONLY

AS FOUR

Used for labelling the garments, industrial-sized rubber bands were printed with all the sizes and cuts. "One label for all."

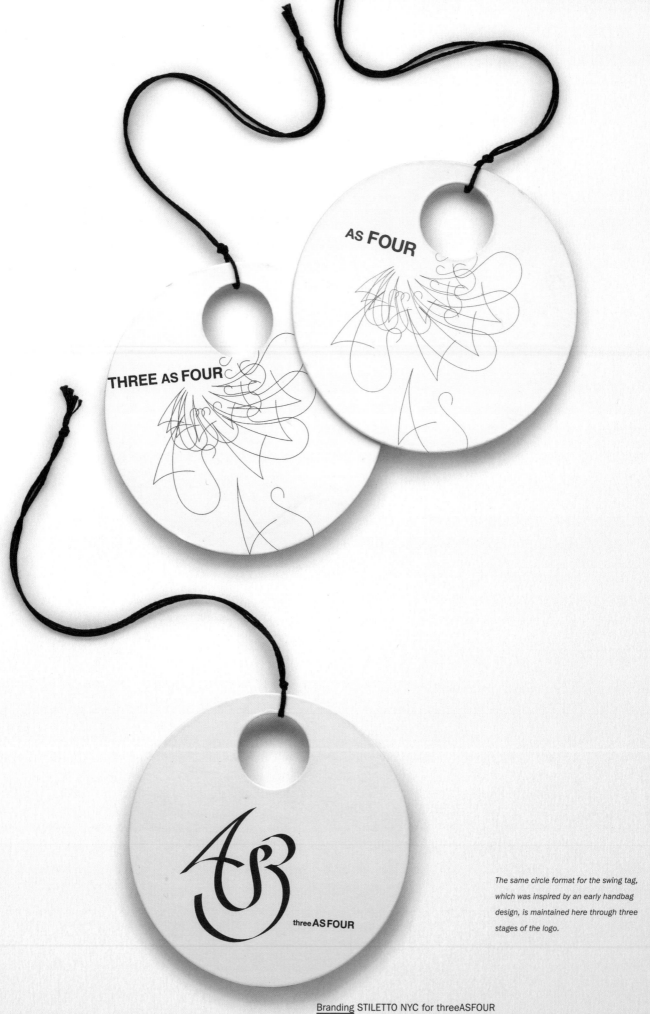

The same circle format for the swing tag, which was inspired by an early handbag design, is maintained here through three stages of the logo.

Branding STILETTO NYC for threeASFOUR

Stiletto manipulate the size and cropping
of the logo with confidence. This was a book
project that had several, different-sized
booklets; as the covers became smaller
the logo was cropped more. With black foil
stamping on black paper the Autumn/Winter
2008/09 collection invitation saw the logo
completely integrated into the illustration.

threeASFOUR
FALL WINTER 2008
COLLECTION
SATURDAY FEBRUARY 2ND 6.00 PM
135 WEST 18TH STREET
NEW YORK CITY
RSVP 212.228.4006 OR
THREEASFOUR@COMPANYAGENDA.COM

INVITATIONS

ANNOUNCE, BUILD ANTICIPATION AND GRANT ADMISSION TO SEASONAL FASHION PRESENTATIONS.

INTRODUCTION

ENTRY TO THE CATWALK SHOW IS ONLY GRANTED FOR A SELECT FEW AND, AS SUCH, INVITATIONS TO THESE EVENTS ARE RESTRICTED AND SIGNIFY THE EXCLUSIVITY OF THE FASHION INDUSTRY. BEYOND THE PRACTICAL DETAILS OF THE EVENT, THIS IS AN OPPORTUNITY TO STIMULATE THE INTEREST IN THE PRESENTATION – FOR THE AUDIENCE, THE EXPERIENCE BEGINS WITH THE INVITATION. THE INVITATION MUST BE RELEVANT TO THE COLLECTION BUT IT MUST BE ABSTRACTED TO AVOID REVEALING TOO MANY DETAILS. USUALLY VERY FEW INVITATIONS ARE PRODUCED, PROVIDING THE GRAPHIC DESIGNER WITH THE CHANCE TO EXPLORE SPECIALIST PRODUCTION TECHNIQUES. AMBITIOUS, CREATIVE SOLUTIONS INEVITABLY HANG UPON LAST-MINUTE DATE AND TIME CONFIRMATION. EVERYTHING MUST COME TOGETHER IN THE TIGHTEST OF ALL FASHION DEADLINES. THE MOST SUCCESSFUL INVITATIONS TRANSCEND THEIR BRIEF PURPOSE AND BECOME CHERISHED MEMENTOS OF THE EVENT.

HOW DO YOU KNOW WHEN SOMETHING IS GOOD?
I WOULD SAY... I WISHED THAT I HAD CREATED IT[66]
WHEN BOTH OF US LIKE IT[70] *I DON'T THINK SO*[70]
THERE'S NOT A FORMULA; IT'S JUST A FEELING YOU
HAVE[78]   I USUALLY JUST ASSUME IT'S BAD UNTIL
I HEAR OTHERWISE[80]   OUR AIM IS TO ALWAYS MEET
A CLIENT'S BUSINESS NEEDS, YET SURPASS
EXPECTATIONS OF WHAT CAN BE ACHIEVED
CREATIVELY[84]   I FEEL IT IN MY FINGERS. A SUDDEN
ENTHUSIASM POPS UP, AND EVEN WHEN IT STILL
LOOKS HORRIBLE, I KNOW I'M ON THE RIGHT TRACK[86]
WHEN IT APPEARS EFFORTLESS[90]   IF IT DOESN'T LOOK
LIKE SOMETHING YOU HAVE SEEN OR DONE BEFORE[94]
I JUST DO[98]   WE JUDGE SOMETHING WHETHER THE
OBJECT IS CLEAR OR NOT[102]   I CAN SEE IT IN THEIR
EYES[106]   GUT FEELING. YOU JUST K N O W, YOU
KNOW[110]   THINK THAT'S AN INTUITIVE THING. I DON'T
THINK THAT'S SOMETHING I CAN EXPLAIN[118]   YOU
KNOW SOMETHING IS GOOD WHEN IT GIVES YOU
A LITTLE TINGLE DOWN THERE[120]   WHEN YOU SEE
SOMETHING GOOD, YOU FEEL GOOD[126]   IF IT FULFILS
ITS PURPOSE, THE CLIENT IS HAPPY AND YOU ARE
PROUD TO PUT YOUR NAME TO IT[130]   I ALWAYS TEND
TO GO WITH MY GUT FEELING, CONSTANTLY ASKING
MYSELF "DO I LIKE WHAT I HAVE DONE, AM I EXCITED
BY MY IDEAS?" IF THE ANSWER IS YES, THEN THERE
IS A GOOD CHANCE THAT THE CLIENT WILL LIKE WHAT
YOU'VE DONE. YOU JUST DO WHAT YOU THINK IS
RIGHT AND HOPE THEY AGREE WITH YOU![136]

ABOUD CREATIVE for PAUL SMITH

Although the success of London-based Aboud Creative has been sustained by an extensive range of clients for more than two decades, they are immediately associated with their work for Paul Smith. The longevity of the association with him, and the subsequent volume of work, is unparalleled in the flippant fashion industry. When Alan Aboud graduated in 1989, the recession meant there was little chance of gaining immediate employment. Relieved of the pressure to deliver an industry-ready portfolio, he focused on a personal brand of typography and was somewhat surprised to be called in by Smith after his degree show. "My work was totally non-fashion, non-figurative, it was the real antithesis of what you would expect. But Paul has a knack of choosing the 'wrong' person. It is an obtuse but intuitive way of working." Smith appointed Aboud to produce his print materials, and as the position required only a few days a week, Aboud balanced the work with other freelance projects. Without any real intention of starting a studio, he took over a desk with Sandro Sodano and within one year the pair had formed a loose creative partnership that played a vital creative role in the growth of the Paul Smith brand.

Smith is drawn to exploring his broad creative potential perhaps more than he is drawn to fashion itself. While known for his colourful twist on modern men's tailoring, he has expanded his brand to reflect the extensive range of what inspires him and his unique personal vision. In direct contrast to the trend-focused fashion industry the Paul Smith brand is based on individuality rather than a prescribed definition of style.

to produce 70 invitations for any other fashion brand." Charting the organic growth of Paul Smith and Aboud Creative, the invitations represent a small proportion of the vast commissions the relationship has generated over the years.

Aboud is increasingly involved in non-commercial projects for Paul Smith that greatly enhance the creative collaboration. "The line has been blurred between what they do and what we do." This intimacy and personal touch is paramount to the Paul Smith brand and business practice. As a result of its longevity and shared experience, the relationship has become incredibly close. Smith's intuitive hunch to employ Aboud has produced an iconic body of work and a lasting friendship.

www.aboud-creative.com
www.paulsmith.co.uk

Aboud admits that initially, due to the fledgling nature of their relationship, "there was a tiny bit of mistrust and a tiny bit of resistance to ideas". In time this developed into an intimate professional collaboration based on mutual respect. While the relentless pursuit of new ideas in fashion has at times threatened the relationship, Aboud has managed to weather the storm and secure his position. Aboud Creative now function almost as the in-house creative team yet remain autonomous. This intimacy skews the conventional designer/client relationship as they are completely integrated into the core of the brand. "I can't explain why or how we are still working together, it's just a bond we have. There are no written briefs; it's usually just a picture or a scribbled note. I know intuitively what he wants and I can just get on with it. I think that is what makes him happy."

For the Paul Smith label, the process of producing invitations begins up to four months in advance of the main catwalk presentation. Their design is shifted by continual discussions between Aboud and Smith. "The whole purpose of the invitation is to create interest, communicate the details and provide a hint of what will be seen or where it will be seen." Invitations are usually based on an iconic print, the venue, a dominant colour theme or a mixture of these components. Their success comes down to open dialogue and the freedom to run with an idea without preconceptions.

Rather than specific invitations being associated with any stand-out seasons, it is their collective impact that is truly inspiring. "There is still a freshness to all of them. They are promoting the same thing but when they are grouped together there is a huge variety of imagery and typography. Paul Smith is a company that never stagnates; I think I would struggle

Across seasonal catwalk presentations and a range of Paul Smith diffusion lines, the sheer volume of invitations of the 20-year relationship is impressive. Intimately linked with each collection, the invitations utilize a broad range of production techniques. A selection is presented on the following pages.

MONDAY 22ND SEPTEMBER
EMPRESS STATE, 55 LILLIE ROAD, LONDON
SW6 1TR. PRESS ENQUIRIES CONTACT:
EMMA HORLEY, TELEPHONE: +44 20 7257
EMMA.HORLEY@PAULSMITH
ENQUIRIES CONTACT: STUART
NE: +44 20 7257 6662
STUART.HOWIE@PAULSMITH
BRING THIS INVITATION WITH
ITE IS STRICTLY NON-TRANS

Paul Smith

PAUL SMITH HAS THE PLEASURE
OF INVITING YOU TO HIS
SPRING SUMMER 2009 SHOW
MONDAY 15TH SEPTEMBER
AT 7.00PM

CLARIDGE'S, BALLROOM ENTRANCE
BROOK STREET, MAYFAIR, LONDON W1

Paul Smith requests the pleasure of
your company to celebrate the openi
Paul Smith Los Angeles
8221 Melrose Avenue
Thursday 8th December 2005
Drinks 8-11pm. Kindly respond to:
cindy.vieira@paulsmith.co.uk
or bluPRint: 310 281 8078

Smith
WOMEN 2001 Fashion show
House (Embankment entrance) WC2
On Monday 25th September at 6.30pm
Please bring this invitation
with you

Paul Smith autumn winter 2006

67

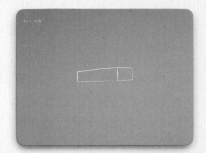

PAUL SMITH WOMEN SPRING SUMMER 2004
MONDAY 22ND SEPTEMBER 2003 AT 10.45 AM
EMPRESS STATE, 55 LILLIE ROAD, LONDON
SW6 1TR. PRESS ENQUIRIES CONTACT:
EMMA HORLEY, TELEPHONE: +44 20 7257 6665
E-MAIL: EMMA.HORLEY@PAULSMITH.CO.UK
SALES ENQUIRIES CONTACT: STUART HOWIE
TELEPHONE: +44 20 7257 6000
E-MAIL: STUART.HOWIE@PAULSMITH.CO.UK
PLEASE BRING THIS INVITATION WITH YOU.
THIS INVITE IS STRICTLY NON-TRANSFERABLE.

PAUL SMITH WOMEN

AUTUMN WINTER 2003

Paul Smith has the pleasure of inviting
you to his Autumn Winter 2003 fashion show.

THE ZIPPO BUILDING
12-28 WOOD LANE
LONDON W12 7DT
WEDNESDAY 19TH FEBRUARY
AT 10.45 AM

– London press enquiries contact:
Emma Horley, Paul Smith Press Office.
Telephone + 44 20 7257 6665
Facsimile + 44 20 7240 1297
E-mail: emma.horley@paulsmith.co.uk

– Please bring this invitation with you.
This invite is strictly non-transferable.
Identification may be required.

Paul Smith requests the pleasure of
your company to celebrate the opening of
Paul Smith Los Angeles
8221 Melrose Avenue
Thursday 8th December 2005
Drinks 8-11pm. Kindly respond to:
cindy.vieira@paulsmith.co.uk
or bluPRint: 310 281 8078

PAUL SMITH WOMEN
SPRING / SUMMER 2005

PAUL SMITH AUTUMN WINTER 10

PAUL SMITH HAS THE PLEASURE
OF INVITING YOU TO HIS
SPRING SUMMER 2009 SHOW
MONDAY 15TH SEPTEMBER
AT 7.00PM

CLARIDGE'S, BALLROOM ENTRANCE,
BROOK STREET, MAYFAIR, LONDON W1

PAUL SMITH WOMEN AUTUMN WINTER 2004

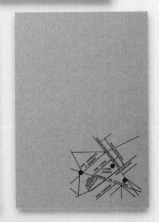

PAUL SMITH
AUTUMN /
WINTER 03

SUNDAY 26TH JANUARY 2003
AT 5.00PM
LYCEE CARNOT
145 BOULEVARD MALESHERBES
75017 PARIS

148-5 = 600

AUTUMN WINTER 2007
FASHION SHOW

TUESDAY FEBRUARY 13TH AT 10.30AM

Paul Smith

SS 08   01 07 07

Paul Smith has the pleasure of inviting you to his
Spring Summer 2008 Fashion Show
on Sunday 1st July 2007 at 4pm

Musée de l'Homme
17 Place du Trocadéro
75016 Paris

Please bring this invitation with you.
This invitation is strictly non-transferable,
identification may be required.
Cette invitation strictement personnelle
vous sera demandée à l'entrée.

Press: Sophie Boilley, Paul Smith Ltd
t. +33 1 53 63 13 19 f. +33 1 53 63 13 24

<u>Invitations ABOUD CREATIVE for PAUL SMITH</u>

paul
smith
spring
summer
two
thousand
and
seven

Paul Smith

paul smith has the
pleasure of inviting
you to his
spring summer two
thousand and seven
fashion show
at: école nationale
supérieure des
beaux arts, 14 rue
bonaparte, 75006
paris, sunday 2nd july
2006 at 17h. please
bring this invitation
with you. this
invitation is strictly
non-transferable,
identification may
be required. cette
invitation strictement
personnelle vous
sera demandée à
l'entrée.

press: sophie boilley,
paul smith limited
t. +33 1 53 63 13 19
f. +33 1 53 63 13 24

PAUL SMITH
presents
AUTUMN
WINTER 2008
FASHION SHOW
SUN 20TH JAN 17h
LIVE AT
CARROUSEL DU LOUVRE, SALLE LENÔTRE
99 RUE DE RIVOLI, 75001 PARIS

invitation

Paul Smith

PLAYERS
PAUL SMITH WOMEN SPRING SUMMER TWO THOUSAND AND TWO
ONLY

Paul Smith
WOMEN

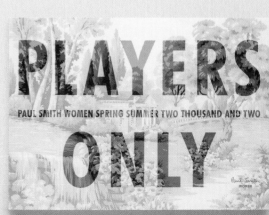

ANTOINE+MANUEL for
CHRISTIAN LACROIX

In an exercise in contrast, Antoine+Manuel apply layered textures, geometric forms and detailed illustrative gestures to build their refined yet chaotic universe. Fluctuating between slick computer graphics and intricate handwork, they also often combine the two to increase the complexity of the results. They exploit an illusion of depth and have had enormous success translating their personal vision from graphic design to wallpaper, furniture and interiors. Custom letterforms are seamlessly integrated into their distinctive illustrative aesthetic, which often resembles blood vessels or electrical circuits. A sinister playfulness runs through their work, supported by an abundant use of colour and texture. Humour is fundamental to their personalities and practice but their ability to transform creativity into entertainment is the real innovation of their practice.

Following graduation in 1993, college friends Antoine Audiau and Manuel Warosz opened their Paris studio. After an initial period they were established enough to become more selective about their clients and began investing time in personal work that would define their visual language. Their enthusiasm has not wavered over the years as they remain adamant that "pleasure comes first, not business!". Their influences on each other are complementary and combine with great effect; for this reason, they have remained independent, apart from the recent addition of interns to facilitate more large-scale projects.

Directly informed by the requirements of each client, their work is identifiable through their high-impact use of form and colour. "For each project we invent a system, a kind of universe." Their style is so distinctive that when commissioned to reinvent the visual language of their clients they are encouraged to impart their own unique aesthetic. Lavish, luxurious and illustrative, their results always leave a lasting impression – they are a perfect match with the fashion industry. "Fashion gives you a certain freedom of creation, you can experiment, play, have fun. Fashion constantly changes, so you can dare, you don't always have to be 'right'." Audiau studied fashion design in college and it has been a continual part of the Antonie+Manuel practice. From a branding exercise for Christian Lacroix in 2002, they have built a close professional relationship and impressive body of work. Known for his extravagant creative fantasies, Lacroix embraces fashion as a lifestyle rather than a profession, an attitude to work that is clearly paralleled by Antoine+Manuel. The success and longevity of the relationship is indicative of their "mutual confidence and respect," says Audiau.

The invitations bring together Antoine+Manuel's flair and exquisite production values to reflect a pinnacle of the fashion industry. "We have access to every existing printing technique, from traditional to hi-tech." Antoine+Manuel are clearly stimulated by the trust placed in them and consistently add explosive dimensions to the Lacroix catwalk. The invitations become coveted souvenirs of attending a show, a tangible gift elevated by the exclusivity of haute couture.

Antoine+Manuel are motivated by the seasonal nature of fashion, and insist: "Each new invitation must be better than the previous one." While the invitations collectively represent an eye-watering education in print production, the embellishments are always completely integrated.

Antoine+Manuel's ability to balance a multitude of production and visual elements to create a single cohesive message is exceptional. Conscious of the illustrious tradition of haute couture, they are not afraid to ruffle the establishment and present a notably progressive vocabulary for Lacroix.

While the relationship with Christian Lacroix has been mutually rewarding, they do not feel this is a direct result of a shared creative background. They emphasize the importance of open-minded, inspiring clients who foster a positive working dialogue. Enthusiasm is also vital and they stress that an emotional connection to their work is essential. Antoine+Manuel's boundless creativity and innovative production techniques ensure the results are always memorable as they extend their designs beyond simple communication to an aesthetic experience.

With multiple iterations upon the same seasonal aesthetic, a substantial complexity is built into each invitation 'package.' The Autumn/Winter 2008/09 Haute Couture invitation consisted of individual cards functioning as the main invitation, RSVP and notes on the influence of the collection. Guests of the catwalk presentation also receive a booklet with detailed notes on each look. In addition to an array of specialist production techniques, an innovative, mottled, metallic blocking technique was applied to the Christian Lacroix logo. "Most of the time we are really happy with the realizations, as we tend to work with the best printers, engravers, stampers here in Paris, each of them in its category chosen for its skills. It's printing's haute couture."

www.antoineetmanuel.com
www.christian-lacroix.fr

hristian Lacro

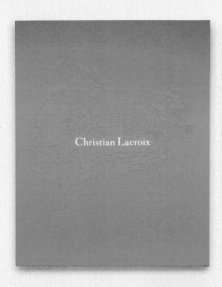

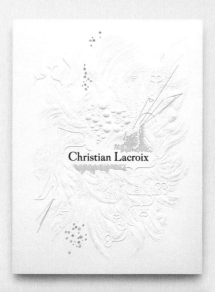

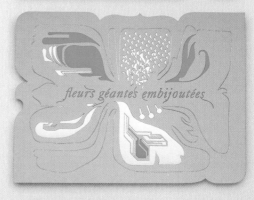

Selection of Haute Couture invitations between Autumn/Winter 2002/03 and Spring/Summer 2006.

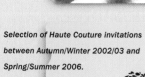

With subtle variations in size, both Haute Couture and Prêt-à-Porter invitations are approximately A5. This is a selection of Haute Couture invitations between Autumn/Winter 2006/07 and Spring/Summer 2009. "Each new invitation must be better than the previous one."

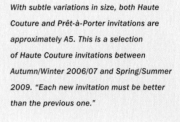

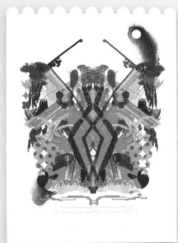

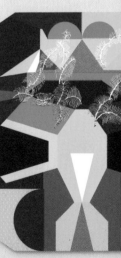

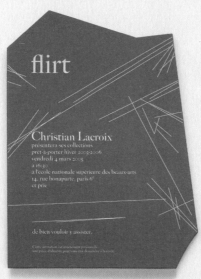

flirt

Christian Lacroix
présentera ses collections
prêt-à-porter hiver 2005-2006
vendredi 4 mars 2005
à 16:30
à l'école nationale supérieure des beaux-arts
14, rue bonaparte, paris 6e
et prie

de bien vouloir y assister.

Cette invitation est strictement personnelle.
une pièce d'identité peut vous être demandée à l'entrée.

Christian

Christian Lacr
COLLECTION PRÊT-À-PO
AUTOMNE-HIVER 2007
28 FÉVRIER 2007

"We have access to every existing printing technique, from traditional to hi-tech." Selection of Prêt-à-Porter invitations between Autumn/Winter 2005/06 and Spring/Summer 2009.

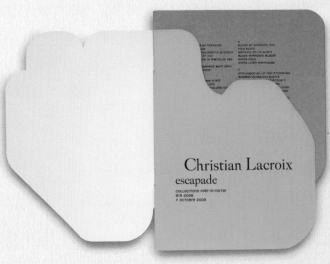

Selection of Prêt-à-Porter invitations and credit booklets between Spring/Summer 2006 and Autumn/Winter 2009/10.

Christian Lacroix
escapade
collections prêt-à-porter
été 2006
7 octobre 2005

Christian Lacroix
collection prêt-à-porter
automne-hiver 2009-2010
6 mars 2009

Invitations ANTOINE+MANUEL for CHRISTIAN LACROIX

For the Prêt-à-Porter Autumn/Winter
2008/09 invitation a folded A3 poster
was also included directly embracing the
collectability of the package. "As Christian
Lacroix is a haute couture and luxury brand,
we are trying to produce precious things,
thinking (maybe it's pretentious) that they
will become a piece of history."

BASEDESIGN for LOEWE

Averse to the limitations of specialization, Base is free from creative and geographical restrictions. Across six cities in five countries, and with five departments, Base has the ability to operate both independently and collectively, with the emphasis on integrated communication. College friends Thierry Brunfaut, Juliette Cavenaile and Dimitri Jeurissen started the studio in Brussels after graduating in 1993. Marc Panero joined in 1996, opening their second office in Barcelona, with Madrid following soon afterwards. The final partner to join was Geoff Cook, when he opened the New York office in 1998, Paris and Santiago offices opened most recently. "The reason is more organic than strategic," says Brunfaut. "Over the years, good opportunities have presented themselves in different locations, and we've seized them." This progressive expansion has drawn additional services to the company: as well as the original graphic design department, BaseDesign, BaseMotion works in animated graphics and film; BaseLab develops custom typefaces; BaseWords writes; BasePublishing publishes and distributes books.

The studio's early relationships in the fashion industry developed through friends. For success Brunfaut emphasizes the importance of creative curiosity and an openness to short schedules. The speed of the industry requires fresh ideas every six months that support the brand but distinguish each season individually. "It is a world that we understand and that affords us freedom and creativity." As such, fashion has been a constant part of the Base roster. While a shared visual background can create greater understanding and mutual appreciation, Brunfaut believes it is important to work with people from different backgrounds.

In 2006 the Madrid office was invited by Loewe to develop a complete identity solution for their 160th anniversary celebration. A distinguished Spanish luxury brand with a heritage that stretches back to 1846, Loewe originated as a purveyor of fine leather goods for the Madrid aristocracy. It has successfully translated the classical values of exquisite craftsmanship into contemporary luxury fashion. Tasked with celebrating such distinctive quality, Base found inspiration in the wide range of logos the label had used throughout its history. An identity system that utilized these marks was developed, and provided the connection between each element of the project. Materials and production techniques were explored in great detail to ensure the result would be compatible with the brand's exclusivity. "The final pieces breathed luxury and style in an appropriate way for the client."

Base believe in the benefits of collective intelligence, and collaboration is fundamental to their internal practice and identity. "Trust is the basic factor." Their geographical spread also requires constant dialogue to inspire innovative solutions that will stimulate their clients' ambitions. Brunfaut is adamant that a good process always leads to a good result. Developing an understanding of the client and their universe ensures the end product is "simple, logical, clear, relevant and communicative". A creative passion flows through every project; and it is this level of clarity and practicality that has been vital to Base's long-term success.

In the rare event of a difference of opinion with clients, Brunfaut is pragmatic. "Force is useless. We always try to make the client understand 'our vision'. Enthusiasm plays a bigger role than stubbornness. Without

a good and understandable concept, well communicated, there is not much to do. Ideas are shared not imposed."

Overall there is a constructive confidence within Base. Their network has created a vast level of experience underpinned by their no-nonsense positive attitude. "Working seriously without taking ourselves seriously," is their philosophy. While the company has a global reach, it maintains a local touch. This flexible approach is perfectly suited to their continual pursuit of challenges initiated by both clients and themselves.

www.basedesign.com
www.loewe.com

"We were able to develop the project without economical restraints in production, we pushed the idea exactly to where we wanted. A special branded ribbon was silkscreened for the project and used throughout the different pieces. The catalogue was a beautiful object-box-bag that used the ribbon as a handle; the invitation used the ribbon as identifying mark; silver foil and screen-printing were used over black cardboard paper, as well as in the invitation." Inscribed by hand, the invitation features silver gilt trimmed edges and was delivered inside a bespoke presentation case with invisible magnetic closure.

MR. Shun Ching Chan

COMMISSIONED WORKS NY for
RACHEL COMEY

Based out of New York, Sean Carmody set up his freelance practice in 2006 before establishing Commissioned Works NY in 2009. He is selective about the projects he takes on, with a particular style of graphic design that demands an extremely high level of mutual trust with his clients. Within the current climate of precision technology, he at times exploits the limitations of production to achieve innovative results. "In some instances we opt for a production technique that may be more of an experiment than an exact science. So from the onset I am prepared to relinquish a degree of control. It's not entirely a roll of the dice. I know roughly what I can achieve, but uncertainty is an equal facet of the project." The fact that there is no guaranteed result seems to heighten Carmody's interest in the whole process.

Rachel Comey translates vintage clothing into contemporary fashion, with abundant quirkiness and a focus on prints and layered textures. Carmody has developed her complete visual communication since 2006, and their relationship demonstrates his integral requirement of respect. "It allows for experimentation and risk-taking. There may be a direction that she or I feel uneasy about but because we trust each other it allows for chance and experimentation." This trust means Carmody has been able to indulge in unpredictable production techniques for some of Comey's projects with greater confidence.

Carmody does not believe that a shared creative understanding, or the fashion industry itself, is particularly accountable for the success of his work for Comey. "It is simply a good collaboration. The fashion aspect is incidental. I think there is a mutual enthusiasm for how things look.

That does not mean they have to be pretty," he says. The manipulation of the conventional definition of beauty is common to both of them: their relationship explores a personalized form of self-expression that is far removed from the polished glamour of fashion. Carmody acknowledges that Comey is important in the creative process but maintains responsibility for his side of the partnership. "Technically she is a client but the relationship functions as well as it does because she is more a collaborator than client."

Although Comey's participation fluctuates depending on the project, she is consistent in her encouragement of Carmody. Highly motivated, he will take the initiative and occasionally present her with unsolicited new ideas and concepts. "I like to create the project, then find an application for it." The equivalent of working backwards from the solution, this proactive approach is indicative of his interest in breaking down the designer/client relationship. While avoiding the conventional parameters of a brief admittedly creates new challenges, the relationship is enhanced as Carmody becomes more active in the design process, which benefits the end results.

Because of his constant pursuit of new challenges, Carmody thrives on the continual cycle of fashion and the focus it requires. Rather than reflect the actual collection, invitations tend to focus on the catwalk experience. Location, music and lighting build directly on the aesthetic of the collection, providing Carmody with a reference point for the invitations. Hesitant to invest too much importance in their long-term value, he admits that if they are special enough, "people hold on to them and invest some value in them. At that point they begin to serve another function."

While Carmody produces innovative solutions, it is his unconventional process that sets him apart. However, equally important are results; he believes that the success of the processes he uses can only be judged by the final product. Rather than over-intellectualize his projects, Carmody prefers to trust his intuition. His work is personal and derived from a refined instinct. In a highly digitalized society, a flexible attitude to the final result creates a more personalized communication, and in some ways reinforces the importance of the message over the physical form it takes.

www.commissionedworksny.com
www.rachelcomey.com

An individual promotion mailer was produced for the shoe collection associated with Spring/Summer 2007. "This season's collection was influenced by the natural world and its mystical qualities. To reflect this we art directed a series of images in which an arrangement of the clothing would conjure up strange occurrences in nature. The partially legible typography reflects this, leaving much of the story a mystery."

from
"THE CLAIRVOYANT CIRCULAR"
- anonymous submission

COSMIC MYSTICISM & OTHER REALLY POWERFUL SHIT

I was seventeen years old. The summer was long and boring. One day while walking home from the beach I noticed a flea market in an open field of grass. I swear it had just appeared out of nowhere because it wasn't there when I walked by earlier. I was curious and thought I could find an addition to my seaside postcard collection. I made my way through the aisles, but found nothing. Then, randomly I heard someone call my name. When I looked up, I noticed a table I hadn't seen before. There was an old man behind the table who motioned for me to come closer. I asked if he had any seaside postcards. He said all he had was a Ouija board, and that I must buy it. It was dusty and cracked, but he still wanted five dollars for it. I said "Two". "Two fifty" he said. So I agreed and he placed it in a plastic shopping bag and I headed home. Later that night, after dinner, my friend and I attempted to work the board. Nothing happened. Although I thought about returning it to the old man, we still kept trying anyway, until late into the night. Finally the wedge began to move from letter to letter. We couldn't understand what the board was telling us, and my friend grew tired and fearful of the the game. She kept accusing me of moving the wedge and decided not to play it anymore. I swore it wasn't me, but she would not touch the board again. For me, the garbled messages only increased my curiosity. I attempted to move the wedge and play the game alone. The first day or two the wedge did not move, but I was determined. Finally, the wedge moved to come alive moving from letter to letter. The messages were finally clear.

"For Spring/Summer 2007 we discussed producing something beautiful from something very modest, a newspaper. Since we had decided on the medium being newsprint, I became interested in what happens when you take something iconic for content (a newspaper) and remove all that content. No amount of quality control could be assured by the printers, so the piece needed to be flexible and we couldn't be precious with the results. We both needed to be flexible with this piece because the production techniques were something of a gamble."

RACHEL COMEY SPRING 2007
ALL WOMEN'S COLLECTION
135 W. 18TH ST. BTWN 6TH & 7TH
MONDAY, THE 11TH AT 3 PM
RSVP PEOPLE'S REVOLUTION
212 501 6019

Invitations COMMISSIONED WORKS NY for RACHEL COMEY

EGELNICK AND WEBB for
HOUSE OF HOLLAND

Toby Egelnick and Malcolm Webb established their London studio in 1999 with the mantra that design should be "intelligent, engaging and memorable". Integrating their experience in the music and fashion industries, their work is very considered with a sophisticated polish that has naturally drawn the attention of the luxury sector. "We work with brands that appreciate a high-end aesthetic and the leverage this adds in terms of both sales and perception," says Webb. The studio has a network of creative collaborators who can be called in for specific projects, allowing its core to remain compact, flexible and creatively focused. Within this structure, teamwork is vital to ensure that Engelnick and Webb's breadth of experience and skills stimulates innovative results. While always focused on the requirements of the client, there is a clear intention to inject a fresh perspective into every project, large or small. This dedication is indicative of an underlying desire to push beyond a client's immediate impression of what is achievable.

Webb believes there is a "synergistic bond" between all creative disciplines and that graphic and fashion design, "track and echo much of the same trends, developing cohesion between the two disciplines". He believes that on most occasions this connection provides a better understanding of the design process and heightens the creative expectations of the fashion client that the design studio must respond to. Webb admits it is a unique priority, tempered only by relatively modest budgets. Egelnick and Webb are able to strike a balance between the creative incentive and financial restrictions and produce particularly inventive results.

Mutual understanding is a basic requirement for any productive creative relationship. "We work closely with the fashion designer to create graphic material that is an extension of their collections," says Webb. The Autumn/Winter 2009/10 invitation for House of Holland was a perfect example of this continuity. The collection was a playful yet refined exploration of colour and tonal variation infused with the raw enthusiasm for fashion and self-reflective humour that is expected from House of Holland. Appropriating one of the basic tools of graphic design, the Pantone chip book, the invitation played directly into the collection yet did not subvert anticipation of the catwalk presentation. Stock from a total of eight books was used: uncoated for the invitations to the show, coated for the party after the presentation. As a bonus, to reinforce their individuality each invitation represented a unique colour palette that became evident when guests arrived at the queue to the venue. The effortless balance of the concept belies its sophisticated execution and the impact a single invitation can have on a fashion show.

One of the key strengths of Egelnick and Webb is that rather than imposing a house style they gain inspiration from content and practise a creative process that builds upon it and delivers a seamless message. As a result, their work cannot be fully appreciated in isolation. "Our aim is to always meet a client's business needs, yet surpass expectations of what can be achieved creatively," says Webb. "There are always interesting possibilities within every new project. Our clients appreciate our approach, which focuses on delivering aesthetically beautiful design that is bespoke, unique and memorable." Undoubtedly, it is an approach that will see Egelnick and Webb continue to move from strength to strength.

www.egelnickandwebb.com
www.houseofholland.co.uk

YOU ARE
INVITED TO
THE HOUSE
OF HOLLAND
AUTUMN/
WINTER 09/10
SHOW,
YOU LUCKY
LUCKY THING.

"We screenprinted the main text of the show and the after party in black over 500 uncoated and 500 coated swatch sheets respectively, with the times, details and sponsor logos on the reverse. The result is a set of invites where only two or three are ever the same, and the job could be described as being printed with 1,050 special colours."

HANSJE VAN HALEM for
ORSON+BODIL

When Hansje van Halem graduated in 2003, a series of well-timed commissions distracted her from looking for a job in a design studio. Based in Amsterdam, her practice focuses on geometric typographic structures in an almost tactile way, yet she has little interest in actual letterforms: "My focus has never been the shape of the letter, but the tint of it." Her work is characterized by the use of highly complex illustrative systems, clearly created by the computer yet retaining residual human quality in the form of imperfections.

While creating a modern world of sharp, graphic forms and texture, surprisingly van Halem looks to the past for inspiration, surrounding herself with old books and generally avoiding the design press. Cautious of the 'graphic designer' label, she considers herself more of a labourer, occupying a traditional role within modern society. Her discovery of the Wacom tablet was pivotal, providing the opportunity to "do manual labour in the computer". She has found a way to reconcile handcraft with technology in a way that is completely original. Without pastiche, she carries the human element into the machine to create something new. "Despite the fact that my letters are made on the computer, I love uneven details, irregularities, visible exhaustion and visible progress in drawings."

Raised by artistic parents, van Halem's childhood was filled with creative possibilities and materials to work with, and these formed her fascination with black and white, textiles, paper and patterns. She is dedicated to free experimentation and builds time into her working day to ensure opportunities for inspiration. Although she is a solo practitioner, she is an advocate of collaboration and regularly teams up with her clients. "On the one hand it is really nice to like your clients, and it makes me happy to communicate with them and produce good work for them. It's like giving gifts and making people happy. On the other hand, it does diffuse the conflict that can make some design so good."

Established in 1988 and relaunched in 2003, Orson+Bodil is a conceptually driven women's fashion label designed by Alexander van Slobbe. In Spring/Summer 2007 a last-minute job to design a 'dossier' and press release was turned over to van Halem. She seized the opportunity, and the success of the small project opened the door for her to design the invitations for the following two seasons. "It's usually a blessing to work for creative clients, because they understand the importance of the freedom they can provide. But sometimes it can also work the opposite way. When I get too much freedom I completely freak out without boundaries. Then I long for the understanding client with strange and unrealistic wishes, when the graphic designer is the expert and able to push beyond expectations. For creative clients, this is expected and harder to achieve." While van Halem admits she is personally disengaged from fashion as a consumer, she sees the connection between fashion and graphic design at street level, fully integrated into life and evolving on a daily basis.

There is a laboured intensity to van Halem's work – a literally visual tension. Process is important to her: she develops rules and systems then invests large amounts of time in the execution of projects, hoping to reap the rewards with the final product. It is an intuitive process that she considers "an ongoing fight in line widths, scale, texture, cluttering and most of all handwriting".

The battle continues as she refines her technique and discovers new applications, a back catalogue of creating tints and gradients with simple black lines.

www.hansje.net
www.orson-bodil.com

orson + bodil
UITNODIGING
zomercollectie
2008

For the Spring/Summer 2008 collection,
a 'dossier' was designed to hold last-minute
notices such as press releases or invitations.
"By cutting a diagonal corner, the content
is visible. Each season employs a different
internal colour that corresponds to the
key colour of the collection." The pattern
references the braiding technique used
in the collection.

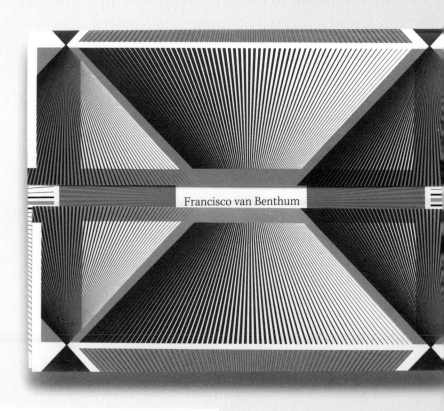

Francisco van Benthum

11 februari 2008
presentatie winter collecties 2008

orson + bodil
&

Francisco van Benthum

u bent van harte uitgenodigd
Het Stadsarchief, gebouw De Bazel,
Vijzelstraat 32, 1017 HL Amsterdam
om 20.00 uur

"To celebrate Alexander van Slobbe's and Fransisco van Benthum's respective twentieth and fifth years in fashion they combined their Autumn/Winter 2008/09 shows and commissioned a joint invitation. The two invitations are folded into one, each separate side is dedicated to the invite for a separate designer."

DRESSCODE: RSVP voor 6 februari:

orson + bodil

JOHN MORGAN STUDIO for
SINHA–STANIC

In the subjective field of graphic design, John Morgan Studio focus exclusively on content – the only constant element. The absence (read abhorrence) of a 'house style' is indicative of this, allowing them freedom to explore new ideas and build bespoke solutions specific to the content of each client. Starting from scratch can be creatively exhausting, yet personal engagement acts as a bridge from research to inspiration, and allows the studio to explore visual and conceptual solutions until a point is reached that leads to an original and effective design. Their refined process and so-called 'modern traditionalist' aesthetic have become their trademark.

Morgan opened his eponymous studio in London in 2000 and has continued to expand modestly in recent years. In 2004 Fiona Sinha and Aleksandar Stanic started their label and for them it was a natural step to employ the services of a mutual friend, Michael Evidon, who had just joined John Morgan Studio. While based on friendship, the relationship has the professional rigour expected from the studio. Evidon acknowledges that the unique visual language of fashion is loaded with its own connotations and interpretations. "There is a graphic language of fashion design, that I think is often confused with graphic design. When there is just some understanding of what you do, there is often misunderstanding. It takes time to develop trust and with friends there are not the same professional boundaries."

John Morgan Studio were initially commissioned to develop a logo, but the success of the first Sinha–Stanic collection required the immediate expansion of the project to include a full suite of print materials and website.

The speed of developments in the fashion industry somewhat diminishes Evidon's engagement with the content, and he sees designing for Sinha–Stanic as a collective exercise. He considers speed a positive influence and an important parallel between the two disciplines. "The fast pace is one of the things I like about fashion and graphic design. I like not knowing what I will be working on in six months."

Establishing a reputation for the subtle balance of draped fabric, Sinha–Stanic developed a harder edge to the collection that seemed to form a closer bond with the logo. The initial intention was to position the new brand as an established label. With time and a growing reputation it has evolved a unique visual aesthetic that is particularly evident in the progression and clarity of the invitations. "As the collections have become tougher and more confident, the graphic language has moved away from image-based solutions drawn from the collection towards bold, type-only posters," says Evidon.

Conscious of budgetary limitations, Evidon focuses on materials to infuse the invitations with added value. "Independent fashion designers operate on tight budgets. There is a misconception that there is all this money in fashion, which is only true up to a point. We look at the material quality of what we are doing: the right weight of paper, the right shade of white, the right printing process." This attention to detail ensures that the end result lives up to the visually demanding fashion industry.

Before each season Evidon visits the Sinha–Stanic studio to discuss the coming collection. "It's too early to see garments, so I look at fabrics or drawings – mostly just what is on their walls, their inspiration, their colour palette." He appreciates the relative simplicity of invitations as stand-alone objects in comparison to other projects, focusing on their materiality yet remaining innovative. However, he admits they can also be challenging as there is no supporting framework, or time for a project to mature. "It is really a completely formal exercise."

With content-driven graphic design, collaboration with the client is of great importance. "It is easy to forget to listen to the client, but it helps so much." Evidon believes that parallels in approach are of greater advantage to the working relationship with Sinha–Stanic than a shared creative background. The extent of their collaboration varies from season to season, a flexible arrangement that reflects the trust between client and studio. The decision-making process is collective to ensure all parties participate and are satisfied with the end product. "Sometimes there is one solution you know from the start will look right, and sometimes there could be twenty to choose from."

A rich vein of humour and self-awareness supports the thoughtful and rational practice of John Morgan Studio. They have found a fine balance between tradition and style that is undoubtedly timeless. Although they are not the obvious choice for a fashion label, their work is refreshing in times of visual trickery and one-upmanship. While fashion is not the core of their business, their collaboration with Sinha–Stanic has translated into a highly enjoyable creative relationship.

Exploiting the possibility of switching foils several times during a single blocking run, four versions of the Autumn/Winter 2007/08 invitation were created, using black, silver, copper and gold. The collection featured geometric metallic sequins that were attached to the garments through small holes. This, and Barney Bubbles' cover for Ian Dury & The Blockheads' album Do It Yourself, *inspired John to use holes cut from the logo as the central typographic feature of the poster.*

www.morganstudio.co.uk
www.stinastanic.com

SINHA-STANIC Autumn Winter 2007-8
3pm, Tuesday 13/2/2007, Victoria House, Vernon Place entrance, Bloomsbury Square, London WC1. Row: Block: Seat:

UK press: Rachel Sinclair, T +44 (0)20 7833 9505. Press: Totem, Kahl de Salvertes, T +33 1 4925 7979. London showroom: easternBlock, Ema Pietina, T +44 (0)20 7436 7345.
Milan showroom: Braveamoda, Maria Iannotta, T +39 025 501 5997. Paris showroom: easternBlock, Ema Pietina, T +33 1 4276 3870. Design: John Morgan studio

SINHA-STANIC Autumn Winter 2007-8
3pm, Tuesday 13/2/2007, Victoria House, Vernon Place entrance, Bloomsbury Square, London WC1. Row: Block: Seat:

UK press: Rachel Sinclair, T +44 (0)20 7833 9505. Press: Totem, Kahl de Salvertes, T +33 1 4925 7979. London showroom: easternBlock, Ema Pietina, T +44 (0)20 7436 7345.
Milan showroom: Braveamoda, Maria Iannotta, T +39 025 501 5997. Paris showroom: easternBlock, Ema Pietina, T +33 1 4276 3870. Design: John Morgan studio

FASHION FORWARD

SWAROVSKI

M·A·C

Invitations JOHN MORGAN STUDIO for SINHA—STANIC

The Autumn/Winter 2006/07 invitation featured the logo blocked in gloss gold foil on the front, an early reference to the metallics that would become increasingly prominent in the Sinha–Stanic collections. The reverse used a bespoke typeface based on the stencil typewriter used on US passports until 2000. The typographic treatment on the predominantly red Spring/Summer 2008 invitation was indicative of the collection's tighter and sharper look. The Spring/Summer 2009 invitation was directly inspired by the use of bold colour gradients within the collection.

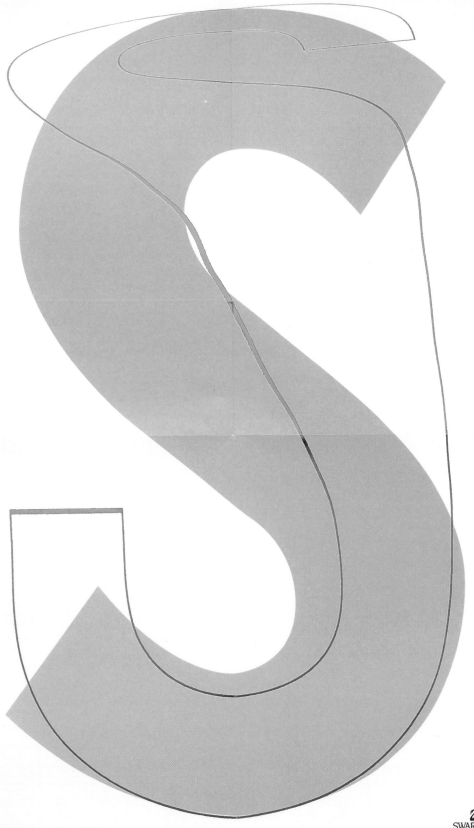

The Autumn/Winter 2008/09 season saw the creation of a semi-diffusion line called 'Stretch' that would focus on jersey pieces. As a literal translation the S letterform was stretched by moving over a photocopier and married with an oxidised copper-toned solid letterform. This treatment was also adapted as the logo for the brand.

SWAROVSKI

M·A·C

On|Off

SINHA–STANIC Autumn Winter 2008–9
10.45, Monday 11/2/2008, On|Off by arrangement with The Royal Academy of Arts 6 Burlington Gardens, London W1

Press London: MODUS, Nick Collins +44 (0)20 7331 1433. Press Paris: TOTEM, Kuki de Salvertes +33 1 4923 7979.
Sales London: RAINBOWWAVE, Maria Lemos +44 (0)20 7352 0002 Sales Paris: RAINBOWWAVE, Maria Lemos +33 1 4703 0960. Design: Michael Evidon

KAREN VAN DE KRAATS for
ANTOINE PETERS

Karen van de Kraats' Amsterdam-based practice follows a predetermined process, dictated by the content. While she does not exclude moments of spontaneous inspiration, her unerring clarity provides a disciplined framework in which to operate. Her systematic decision-making requires complete objectivity: she subscribes to the mantra, "Kill your darlings". This form of creative ruthlessness ensures her work remains relevant to the content and is not influenced by outside trends.

She begins with a brief and detailed discussion with the client, which leads to thorough research to provide references and inspiration. Conceptual links between the results are then formed in the search for an underlying story for the project through form, colour, typefaces and layout. Sketching out these initial concepts clearly indicates their potential success or failure. Ultimately van de Kraats is searching for a solution where "everything is connected with everything else and tells one story. If you cannot explain the concept in a simple way, the concept won't work."

While van de Kraats remains independent, regular collaboration with other creatives is vital to her practice. She acknowledges the necessity for critique, both from clients and contemporaries, to ensure she maximizes the potential of a project and does not lose her perspective on the end product. To avoid alienating the broader audience by overintellectualizing her work, she strives for the clarity required for effective communication. This does not limit her creativity; rather she is able to create a balance of work that is respected by the design community and by the general public.

Stretching back to 2000, the romantic relationship between van de Kraats and Antoine Peters naturally extended into a professional partnership in 2005. While they are fiercely independent within their respective fields, van de Kraats admits, "For us it is obvious that we work together, we don't know it any other way." The instinctive nature of their relationship provides a unique form of fluidity on which they thrive. While adhering to distinct roles, they are able to build a collective ownership that is undoubtedly advantageous to the end result. Their ability to minimize the pressure of balancing a personal and professional life is a tribute to the strength of their relationship.

On the surface, Peters is on the somewhat playful side of the fashion industry, yet through biting juxtaposition his designs offer sharp social relevance. While he develops the concept of a collection and contributes to the art direction, van de Kraats interprets his ideas and refines the graphics into their final state. Rather than working in isolation, Peters and van de Kraats work closely during the development of all visual material. Their goal is to create an end product where graphic design and fashion achieve a "total whole" or "one world where optimism, comfort and elegance meet".

Past experience informs van de Kraats' decisions and builds a deeper understanding of her clients' requirements. "As a designer, if you are not happy with the result, the process can teach you a lot about yourself and your client. Maybe next time you will deal with it differently." Her self-awareness and desire for personal development underline her resolve to renew her process with each new project.

For van de Kraats, success is the development of an original solution, something that is particularly valuable within the visually saturated fashion industry. She believes fashion offers increased creative freedom because of a shared ambition to get the best out of each new project. Creative tension is the catalyst for progress as each party brings unique expertise and priorities to a design. Her strength lies in navigating the possibilities these provide, building on them and shaping them into a direct, unified message.

www.karenvandekraats.com
www.antoinepeters.com

"The Autumn/Winter 2009/10 'I'm with stupid' entrance card was based on one of the collection prints. This invite could be ironed onto your clothes and you could actually 'wear' the invite! This way the visitor was already becoming an active part of the show days before. The actual invite with info about time and place had additional washing and ironing instructions."

PRINTED & SPONSORED BY RIETVELD ERIGRAFIE B.V.
WWW.RIETVELD-SERIGRAFIE.NL

ＴＥＲ FOR THE WORLD!
ＥＰＥＴＥＲＳ presents

A SWEATER FOR THE WORLD!
by ANTOINEPETERS presents

ONE
SWEA-
TER

Friday 26 January 2007
Exhibition   1400 – 2200 HR
Opening word   1600 HR
    Oostelijk Meterhuis (Building 2)
Amsterdam   Westergasfabriek.nl

Information & press   IMAGO FACTORY
+31(0)20 42 12 24
    manuel@imagofactory.com

asweatherfortheworld.com

PHILIPS

AMSTERDAM
INTERNATIONAL
FASHION
WEEK

nuary 2007
    1400 – 2200 HR
rd   1600 HR
    Meterhuis (Building 2)
    Westergasfabriek.nl

ss   IMAGO FACTORY
24
ofactory.com
ld.com

PHILIPS

AMSTERDAM
INTERNATIONAL
FASHION
WEEK

ＴＥＲ FOR THE WORLD!
ＥＰＥＴＥＲＳ

nuary 2007
    1400 – 2200 HR
rd   1600 HR
    Meterhuis (Building 2)
    Westergasfabriek.nl

IMAGO FACTORY
24
ofactory.com

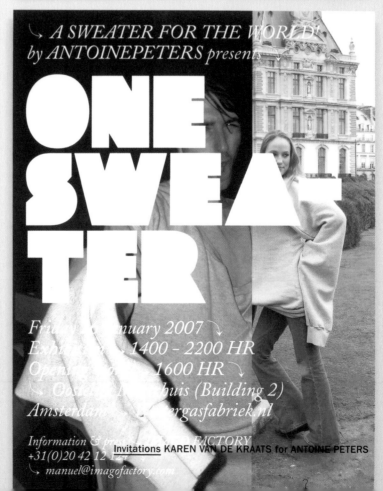

A SWEATER FOR THE WORLD!
by ANTOINEPETERS presents

ONE
SWEA-
TER

Friday 26 January 2007
Exhibition   1400 – 2200 HR
Opening word   1600 HR
    Oostelijk Meterhuis (Building 2)
Amsterdam   Westergasfabriek.nl

Information & press   FACTORY
+31(0)20 42 12 24
    manuel@imagofactory.com

Invitations KAREN VAN DE KRAATS for ANTOINE PETERS

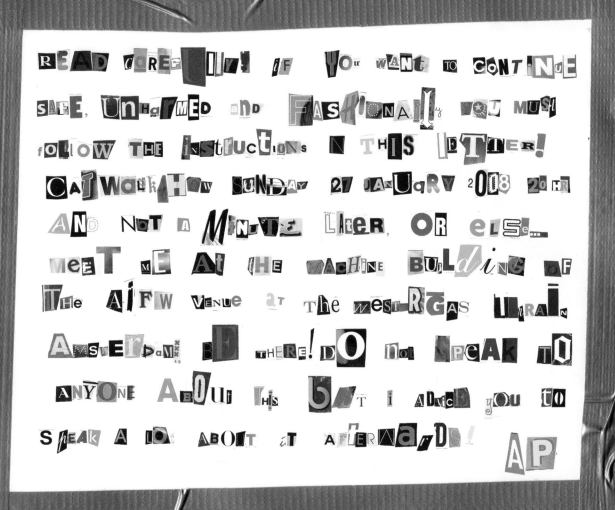

ANTOINE PETERS
S/S 2010
CATWALKSHOW

20 JULY 2009
DOORS OPEN 19.30
START SHOW 20.00

'TURN YOUR FROWN
UPSIDE DOWN.'

Moooi Gallery
Westerstraat 187
1015 MA Amsterdam

ANTOINEPETERS*

Please bring this personal
invitation to ensure entrance.
This invitation admits strictly
one person. Please be advised to
come early because of limited
parking spaces in this area.

SUPPORTED BY

moooi·gallery

un UNITED NUDE ™

For further information please
contact manuel@creampr.nl
or call +31(0)204212124.

WWW.ANTOINEPETERS.COM

REDKEN
FIFTH AVENUE NYC

house of orange

F

ABSOLUT
Country of Sweden
VODKA

GRAPHIC DESIGN BY Karen van de Kraats

OVERNEEK
SOUND

M.A.P.S. in Media

cream
pr

* *PUT* someones *FROWN UPSIDE DOWN* yourself!

OPPOSITE: "This invitation was for the
'One...' exhibition for Autumn Winter
2007/08 featuring the most recent results
of the 'A Sweater for the World' project.
Two different photographs were put together
to emphasize the purpose of the project
in bringing people together from different
walks of life.

"For the Autumn/Winter 2008/09 'Fat
People are Harder to Kidnap' collection
the invite was a ransom letter in which
the recipient was 'politely threatened'
to come to the show, OR ELSE! This was
also integrated into the collection print.
The Spring/Summer 2008 'Le Petit Antoine'
collection played on the idea of clothes
that you've grown out of. This came from
the fact that this was Antoine's very first
big fashion show and dealt with the battle
of staying young at heart. Most recently
the Spring/Summer 2010 'Turn your Frown
Upside Down' collection...."

Invitations KAREN VAN DE KRAATS for ANTOINE PETERS

MULTISTOREY for STÆRK

As the name suggests, London-based Multistorey function on many levels within a broad creative field. Intentionally free from a discernible visual aesthetic, they readily admit to having "some form of identity crisis". This is in part due to a work philosophy that requires every project be treated as a unique exercise to promote innovation while fully satisfying the client's individual requirements. The exploration of materiality and structure is the common thread throughout their body of work: "We have always been interested in the tactility of our projects," says founding partner Harry Woodrow. This goes some way to explaining their success in 3-D experience design, yet is also particularly suitable for the fashion industry, and specifically for Camilla Stærk who is known for her layering of texture.

With a friendship that stretches back over ten years, Stærk was well acquainted with the talents of Multistorey when she started her eponymous label in 2001. In 2006 she left her London company to set up her new label in New York called Stærk. Not only did Multistorey navigate this successfully, but their work throughout this period also adds to the visual record of the transformation.

Usually inspired by the seasons, Stærk explores the tension between antiquity and modernity, leather and lace. Tactility is a key feature throughout her collections and provides immediate common ground for Multistorey to work from. Direct, constructive dialogue between Multistorey and Stærk is vital, even more so now that they are not in the same country. Even while a collection is in development, Stærk is able to clearly articulate the direction it is taking, predominantly through defining her seasonal muse.

It is clear that an overwhelming sense of mutual respect is the key to their success with Stærk, something that possibly cannot be achieved through a more conventional, purely professional relationship.

Although Multistorey do not actively court the fashion industry, they have worked for a range of brands over the years. Woodrow defines the perfect relationship with a fashion designer as being, "When you understand their vision, you like and respect them personally, you enjoy and/or would wear their clothes, they trust you to surprise them, but any input they give actually adds to the end result instead of diluting it." When you can describe your ideal so clearly it is undoubtedly easier to achieve your goals.

This gives Multistorey adequate independent research and development time, together with the assurance that there will be no last-minute changes (except maybe to the time slot).

Multistorey particularly welcome the opportunity invitations provide to produce overtly creative solutions. For a select few, the weeks preceding a fashion week can become an invitation onslaught. With invitations arriving in bulk it is important to immediately spark the interest of the recipient. "Invitations need to be special and precious to stand out," says Woodrow. "You can get a real sense of the personality of the collection, even from a flat piece of card. Due to the rise of digital technology, the value of a well-printed object has increased. It's a lot harder to ignore something in your hand than one in your inbox."

While the seasonal reinvention of fashion was a particular pleasure for Multistorey over the years, Stærk's transition to New York refined her visual direction. Working within a set template, a change of materials and production techniques is the single indicator of the change of season for invitations and lookbooks. Restricted to paper and print process, Multistorey directly interpret the key texture of the collection. Although the creative challenge has been somewhat reduced, the end result is a sophisticated and identifiable message that is indicative of the professionalism of the New York fashion scene. This development was initiated for Autumn/Winter 2007/08, and its collective benefit can now be fully appreciated.

Multistorey keep their focus internal and look beyond the graphic design industry, projecting a calculated and reassuring confidence to their clients.

www.multistorey.net
www.staerk.com

On leather texture paper, random folds
of the Spring/Summer 2006 'Rumours
and Lamentation' collection reference
the faceted structure of the Serpentine
Gallery Pavilion in London where the
presentation was held.

Stærk

Spring 2008

Friday 7th September 2007
7 – 8pm
Show will repeat every fifteen minutes

Scandinavia House
3rd Floor
58 Park Avenue
(between 37th and 38th Street)
New York, NY

RSVP: StaerkRSVP@lindagaunt.com
T: 212 810 2894 ext 105

Stærk

Fall 2007

February 5th 2007 – 2pm
Loft Eleven
336 West 37th Street, 11th Floor
(between 8th & 9th Avenues)
New York, New York 10018

RSVP:
T 212 590 5146
staerk@kcdworldwide.com

Stærk

Spring 2009
The Storyteller

Sunday 7th September 2008, 5 – 6pm
Show times 5pm, 5.20 and 5.40

Bumble and bumble
415 West 13th Street
(Between 9th and 10th Avenue)
New York, NY

RSVP: staerk@lindagaunt.com

*The invitations have been consolidated
into a consistent template. Within this
framework Multistorey focus on translating
the materiality of the collection into the
invitation to create seasonal distinction.*

The Autumn/Winter 2004/05 collection featured lightweight chiffon juxtaposed with metal studs. An onionskin paper was used to simulate the delicacy of the fabric from the collection and when touched makes a very distinct, crisp sound. The translucence was used to echo a pattern of studs used in the collection.

NO DESIGN for ANREALAGE

Tokyo-based NO DESIGN have a disciplined approach and operate with a creative economy that prevents them being distracted from the central message. They focus on precise details of a concept and resist the temptation to overcomplicate. Jun Nakano and Masaya Muto worked together in the design department of the creative studio BLOCKBUSTER, and started NO DESIGN in 2009 to focus exclusively on branding and graphic design. They are searching for a balance between the "extremely concise and the excessively chaotic. We represent the 'No' against valueless and inconsequential 'Design.'"

A year before he launched ANREALAGE, Kunihiko Morinaga was introduced to Nakano and made an immediate impression – the encounter laid the foundation for a professional relationship that began with the company's official launch in 2003. "We simply started to share thoughts and carry out projects together," say NO DESIGN. The conceptually driven label is suited to the gallery yet remains accessible in the retail environment. ANREALAGE re-examines the original beauty of daily life, and each collection is supported by the motto, 'God is in the details'. There are distinct creative parallels with NO DESIGN.

NO DESIGN believe there has been a natural progression between the companies. A bond has developed that provides security and stimulation within the relationship. "We are motivated by the continual exchange of thoughts and ideas with ANREALAGE. As a result, there is a synergy in the creative process." The collective energy and confidence in their work is the sign of a true collaboration. While this level of professional unity cannot be forced, NO DESIGN believe a strong, collaborative relationship can be built with clients who do not have personal creative backgrounds. A complementary aesthetic is important but must be supported by intelligent and incisive dialogue. Although NO DESIGN are thorough and enthusiastic, depending on the situation, they acknowledge the need for a "flexible attitude from the client to produce the best solution".

The fashion industry offers NO DESIGN the specific opportunity to move between two- and three-dimensional solutions. This was particularly evident for the Autumn/Winter 2009/10 collection by ANREALAGE, which directly challenged conventional ideas of form and structure. The garments were so structurally innovative NO DESIGN were able to seamlessly translate this into a pop-up invitation without undermining the catwalk experience. After the event the audience was left with the impression of a completely integrated message.

To be successful, graphic design for the fashion industry must "forget the idea that fashion is high culture and try to appeal to the person who really wears the clothes". This direct approach is achieved by communicating the brand with clarity and honesty. While visual presence is vitally important, NO DESIGN reject a purely emotional response to fashion and choose to build a more rational framework for their creativity. "Design is the pursuit of something logical, there must be a reason." While this does not exclude moments of intuition, they do not overanalyze their process and remain focused on the end result.

www.no-de.jp
www.anrealage.com

"ANREALAGE designed concave-convex clothes for the Autumn/Winter 2009/10 collection. We tried to express this by using the pop-up technique. It is wonderful that we can complement each other with the collaboration/blending between two and three dimensions."

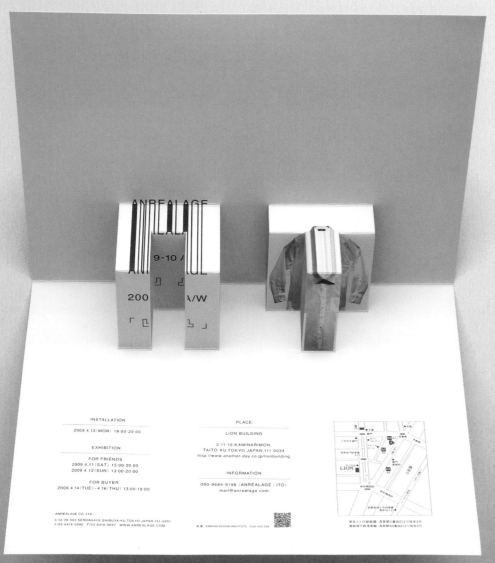

*"We designed the Spring/Summer 2010
invitation by thinking about three main
points. First: to communicate the concept
clearly. Second: to surprise the recipients
and motivate them to visit the collection.
And finally: to make an object that is not
simply two-dimensional."*

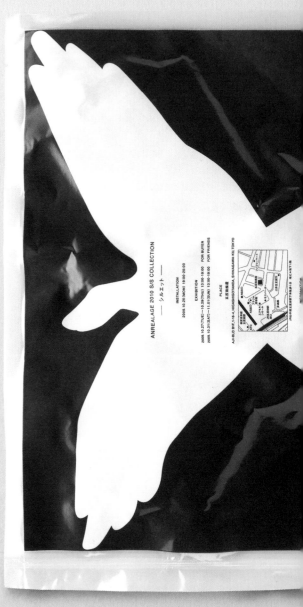

Invitations NO-DESIGN for ANREALAGE

ねえねえ。
……。ねえねえ。なに。……。
だからそう言ってる。そんなこと言
ってたっけ。いつも考えてるよ。分からない。
……すぐに答えを出したがるね。平凡で、穏
和で、寡黙で、異様。色褪せない風景。……。
多いほうがいい。少ないほうがいい。結局同じな
のかもね。立っていた場所。対話の継続。おーい。
……。毎日毎日毎日毎日。……。心にもないこと。届か
ぬ想い。心の拘泥を悟られることを極端に避けるよう
になってしまった。うるさいなあ。……。ねえねえ。……。
ねえねえ。うん。分かった。過剰な均衡は保つので
精いっぱい。ここまでの道のり。鮮やかに残るもの。
色や形。点滅する記憶。きっと晴れていた。丸く
て大きくて優しい。何て弱いんだ。満ち足り
たことなんてない。幸せだと思えばいい。
分かってる。分かってない。目を
閉じる。広がる原風景。
遙か晴る。

"For Autumn/Winter 2007/08 we tried to express multi-layered memories by hiding colourful flowers in a vase. The text in front of the flowers is a list of words like 'monologue', 'silence', 'dialogue' and so on. Those words remind us of a common memory and landscape."

ANREALAGE
2007 A/W COLLECTION

「ハルカハル」

PAOLO BAZZANI for KENZO

Surrounded by the flamboyant Italian fashion capital of Milan, Paolo Bazzani has quietly established a body of work that balances his personal creative vision with the commercial requirements of his clients. He started his independent studio in 2004 and is completely dedicated to the pursuit of creative integration of concept and content.

Bazzani has worked consistently for the fashion designer Antonio Marras throughout his career. Their relationship stretches back to the early 1990s and is built on a close friendship that came before any professional responsibilities. Bazzani admits to an intimacy in the way they work together that can be achieved only through long-term shared experience. In addition to detailed conversations, he uses extensive picture research to clarify his creative direction with Marras. He feels that more than a shared creative language, a commonality in their aesthetic appreciation has sustained the longevity of the partnership.

Immediately after Bazzani graduated, Marras drafted him in to take care of the print requirements for the fashion house in which he was working. In 1999 Marras established his own label, and provided the creative freedom that allowed the collaboration with Bazzani to truly flourish. In 2003 Marras became the artistic director of the Kenzo women's collection, and in 2008 he took over the creative direction for the entire house. Founded by Kenzo Takada in 1970, the label is inspired by the fusion of fashion from around the world, with an expressive colour palette and poetic narrative structures. There is a sweeping romanticism to its collections that produces extravagant catwalk performances.

Intent on translating the creative energy from his eponymous label into Kenzo, Marras automatically looked to Bazzani to continue their collaboration. Conscious of the need to adhere to the Kenzo heritage, Bazzani was able to use his experimentation with the Antonio Marras label in a more structured way. Through their friendship Marras and Bazzani naturally discuss ideas outside the professional requirements at hand. In addition to graphic design, Bazzani has become increasingly involved in catwalk set design. Their shared passion to communicate in a dramatic way means that the Kenzo fashion show has developed into an almost theatrical performance. This has created an opportunity for Bazzani to integrate the invitation directly into the catwalk experience.

Bazzani is involved throughout the process and must be able to adapt as Marras continually refines his central concept. Increasingly busy and based off the fashion map in Sardinia, Marras regularly travels to Milan but the time he spends with Bazzani has become limited. In conjunction with modern technology, the distance between them is overcome by their mutual understanding of their creative process – something that only a long-term relationship can bring. This builds continuity between collections: "Each season is a unique process but we have a consistent way of presenting the main concept," says Bazzani.

While Kenzo traditionally preferred the simplicity of a classical invitation, Bazzani and Marras were able to justify the importance of building anticipation and providing a memento after the event in order to extend the limited catwalk experience. The results are more than disposable instructions; they are limited-edition gifts. The

invitation to the Autumn/Winter 2009/10 menswear collection consists of wooden alphabet blocks that can only create the word 'Kenzo'. To prevent the invitations becoming 'gadgets', Bazzani ensures they do not have a secondary function. Conceptually and structurally elaborate, the invitations have become a trademark of the catwalk season. "This is what we really try to do – create an extension to the experience," says Bazzani.

With his creative remit restricted to fashion journalists and buyers who attend the catwalk show, Bazzani does not have to take the consumer into consideration. Rather than promoting the brand as a whole, he focuses on the single collection. In this context, the reinterpretation of the iconic Kenzo logo is an innovative way to reinforce the message of the collection. While the invitations appear to be produced with no financial restrictions, Bazzani maintains the importance of the idea. Compromises are undoubtedly made, but the invitations are intertwined with the overall concept of the collection and require little justification. Given that the catwalk performance itself is a major investment, their cost is proportionally small and clearly enhances the audience's experience.

Working so closely with Marras for over 20 years has provided Bazzani with greater influence and responsibility. Fashion's constant demand for new ideas means it is undoubtedly difficult to maintain a creative relationship within the industry. Bazzani has risen to the challenge and continues to move from strength to strength, supported by his close friendship with Marras.

www.paolobazzani.it
www.kenzo.com

"I started to personalize the logo of every collection for the Antonio Marras label. We proposed this to Kenzo who were a little worried but soon understood we were not destroying the logo but reinforcing the concept of the show. Everyone invited already knew the logo very well so we can play with this." The Russian-themed Autumn/Winter 2009/10 collection was the first menswear collection for Kenzo by Antonio Marras. Printed on wooden blocks, each letter of the Kenzo name was used to convey the breadth of Russian inspiration for the collection – K for Kandinsky, N for Nabakov, Z for Zhivago, etc.

Invitations PAOLO BAZZANI for KENZO

WILD FLOWERS

❧ NOTEBOOK ❧

Kenzo

printemps été 2009

Samedi 4 octobre 2008 - 10h30

Carreau Du Temple
3 rue Dupetit Thouars - Paris 3ème

Calcéolaires Ligneuses Hybrides

notes

Pentstemon Hybrides

Acacia Rupicola

Service de presse

Adriano Rossi
Elisabetta Pollastri

T. 01 73 04 21 94
F. 01 73 04 21 93

arossi@kenzo.fr

The Spring/Summer 2009 collection is a perfect example of the integration between the invitation and set design of the catwalk presentation. "I wanted to put a butterfly inside the book, so I started with the idea of using a children's pop-up and collector's books. Graphic design usually only concerns itself with two dimensions but for me it is very important to consider the three-dimensionality."

Invitations PAOLO BAZZANI for KENZO

invitation nominative exigée à l'entrée

PAUL BOUDENS for
HAIDER ACKERMANN

Ever since the Antwerp Six burst on to the international fashion scene in 1988, the modest and relatively small Belgian city has played a pivotal role in contemporary fashion; competition is strong within its creative industry and fashion remains the undisputed champion. While Paul Boudens originally set out to be a fashion designer, he now maintains a pragmatic relationship with the industry, content to exist in a supporting role. "I love working 'in the shadow' of a fashion designer, helping to expand their vision, and at the same time doing my own thing for them." With his fervent, emotionally charged work, Boudens has stepped out of the shadow and established his own global reputation.

The creative demands and impossible deadlines of fashion are a perfect match for Boudens. "I love the sheer speed of things. You have to work fast, assignment after assignment; there's a lot of variety with the seasons changing." He operates with a constant sense of urgency, adamant that dwelling too long on a project can breed indecision and boredom.

Contrary to the perpetual reinvention of fashion, Boudens has no interest in trends, preferring the greater challenge of timelessness. He is spontaneously creative, and relies on instinct to guide the direction of each project. "I have no theories about my work. I can only say how I work, and how I came to do what I do. I absolutely hate 'concepts' so I never over analyze things. It's fashion, not science."

Boudens is creatively self-reliant, a bona fide one-man operation – a fact that is disguised by his prolific output. While the burden of solitude can creep in, he is so accustomed to working alone that he no longer has the desire to be part of a studio environment. He admits this is partly to ensure complete control over the end result, but Boudens' talent lies in the sense of intimacy in his work. His personal touch is as distinctive as his fingerprint. Such finesse cannot be entrusted or taught to another individual. Anyone who employs Paul Boudens will get Paul Boudens.

Although his isolation in his studio inhibits conventional collaboration, Boudens values close professional relationships with his clients. Based on a friendship stretching back to the late 1990s, as art director of the biannual fashion title *A Magazine*, Boudens seized the opportunity to install himself as the guest curator for the third issue in 2005. Although both men were somewhat apprehensive initially, their professional relationship was highly successful and they naturally moved on to the Haider Ackermann brand, which is an ongoing project. Although Ackermann is now based in Paris, he and Boudens speak directly about their projects.

Invitations to the Haider Ackermann collections maintain consistency through their uniform dimensions and thickness and weight, while seasonal variations are shown through variable materials, processes and typography. Ackermann's signature muted tones and seductive textures are skilfully reflected each season by Boudens. He has refined the art of translating the vision of the fashion designer while leaving room for his own personal touch. "I think I'm quite good at 'reading' their universe, and schizophrenic enough to adapt myself to their world. In the end you can see that I made it, so it's a perfect marriage."

Honest about the financial limitations of the fashion industry and the ominous trend for the budget to be of primary importance, Boudens is happy to exercise a 'less is more' aesthetic. Any lack of funds is met with inventive dedication to extract the most out of the project. His creative investment is 100 per cent. He puts a great deal of personal energy into every project, and admits that he is despondent when he sees his invitations carelessly discarded at the entrance to a catwalk show. Yet he has a strong sense of humour and self-awareness, supported by a quick wit that turns the negative into the positive. This optimism is best explained by his belief that "The next job is always the nicest".

www.paulboudens.com
www.haiderackermann.be

Using a standard envelope format and maintaining a consistent design approach, Boudens infuses every invitation with the personality of the collection, employing a variety of embossing and foils on very thick board.

PAUL BOUDENS for YOHJI YAMAMOTO

Tension is a continual presence in the work and practice of Paul Boudens. He instinctively fuses incompatible materials and ideas into cohesive examples of communication: complex and simple, rough and smooth, radical and conventional. Because he is not distracted by passing trends, these continue to look as fresh as the moment they were created. It is clear that Boudens executes precise control over the balance between contemporary and classic.

Such skills are highly valued in the fashion industry and it comes as no surprise that in 2003 Boudens attracted the attention of Yohji Yamamoto. Fascinated equally by balance and contrast, Yamamoto embraces the flawed, yet expresses such refined complexity in his silhouettes that they become precise exercises in simplicity. He has successfully bridged the fashions of East and West while satisfying both his artistic inspiration and commercial necessities. The underlying similarities of practice between Boudens and Yamamoto provide a solid and fertile base for their constructive partnership.

Fulfilling the insatiable desire for the 'new' while in pursuit of the eternal seems at odds with the trend-led fashion industry, and the challenge this poses is fundamental to the work of Boudens and Yamamoto. The value of his work cannot be fully appreciated in the moment; time must pass for it to become clear. Boudens admits, "My dream is to make timeless work, even though that is impossible."

Although he is part of an industry that is becoming dominated by the digital, Boudens is committed to maintaining the human element in his work. He refuses to be restricted by the computer, and impacts physically on his projects through a range of processes. While it is not always possible, Boudens strives to find ways to imprint his work with the mark of a human, not a "robot". "I have my own way of working things out on the computer. I have to look for a solution for my incompetence. That's what I want to keep. I do not want to become a computer nerd, the life would go out of my work."

Although Boudens wanted to be a fashion designer at the start of his career, he is not completely enamoured with this sector of the creative industry. He studied language and communication before settling on graphic design, and it is clear that these early interests provided him with sensitivities and perspectives that have been extremely valuable for his career. He believes creativity, not fashion, needs to be the common language in order to produce innovative work. "But sometimes it's important that the graphic designer has a good sense of fashion."

An intricate web of graphic designers is employed to maintain the various brands under the Yohji Yamamoto umbrella. The Paris office mediates the design process for Boudens, and works closely with him to develop presentations that are sent to Yamamoto in Tokyo. Both men are reclusive professionally, and the removed critique process satisfies Bouden's independent desire to communicate with his clients through ideas. "I like short briefings and despise long meetings... just let me loose with it." At his best when left to his own devices, Boudens has earned this rare creative luxury from his clients. This is in part because he single-handedly completes the work, and clients trust his instincts and feel secure in the fact that he will personally execute the final product.

www.paulboudens.com
www.yohjiyamamoto.co.jp

With a relationship that stretches back more than six years, there is mutual confidence in the relationship between Boudens and Yamamoto.

Contrary to the exclusivity of the fashion show, Boudens produces post-catwalk invitations to view the new collection when it is available in showrooms. Rather than avoiding too much detail about the collection, these seasonal invitations promote both its aesthetic and the garments. While not as comprehensive as a lookbook, they are intended to identify the key looks of the season. Boudens has explored a range of materials and processes. "Some seasonal cards were splashed with red paint; some were printed on beautiful pinstriped paper; others had stickers; embossed logos; little plastic overlays with a silk-screened image; others were overprinted twice, some printed on cardboard, had stitching, folded out." Collectively the cards become desirable mementos; void of the practicalities of conventional invitations, their collectability seems enhanced by the impression that they are personalized.

As happens in the world of high fashion, Boudens has the ability to transform the functional into the collectable. He admits to an artistic approach to the commercial nature of graphic design, but remains clear that he is employed to communicate with consumers and would not consider himself an artist. He exhibits an insightful perspective on his own practice and, importantly, his clients. Operating outside the restricted longevity of trends ensures that his solutions are as close to timeless as possible.

"For me working for Yohji Yamamoto was a marriage made in heaven. Especially in the beginning, I was able to fully use my range of skills: the painting, the hand-made feeling, classic typography, gorgeous paper choices and perfectionist finishing."

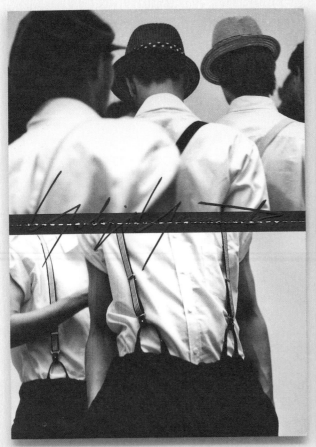

With central perforations these A5 cards
were delivered in translucent metallic
envelopes. Boudens invests heavily
in the materiality of each project.

Invitations PAUL BOUDENS for YOHJI YAMAMOTO

115

Y's for men
YOHJI YAMAMOTO

Y'S FOR 2S.MEN YOHJDU YAMAMOTO AUTUMN WINTER
2003 .42 2004
.42 .01 2003 .42 21 .42 2004 .936
FRANCE.FOR 2S.MEN RUE SAINTS-PERES PARIS 01 .42 21 .48 .56
RUE DES SAINTS-PERES 75001 PARIS 01 45 .48 .48 .258
GALERIES LAFAYETTE 40, BOULEVARD HAUSSMANN 75009 PARIS 01 45 44 63 .200
LE BON MARCHE 24, RUE DE SEVRES.PARIS 01 45 48 34 .145
3. RUE FABRON.13100 AIX-EN-PROVENCE 04 42 27 79 .103
24. RUE LONGCHAMP 06000 NICE 04 93 61 87 21 .61
24. RUE DES ARTS 31000 TOULOUSE 04 05 93 61 13 .65
DENMARK: GAMMEL 31000 1117 COPENHAGEN K1AB 33 08 70 93 .288
UK: SELFRIDGES 400 MONT 10 STREET LONDON W1A K1AB 33 08 70 08 377 377 .377

116

Postcard-sized images are placed in printed plastic sleeves creating a very physical, layered collage. Boudens emphasizes the human aesthetic in his work and is dedicated to achieving the desired effect. "Whatever it takes, I don't care, it's the result that counts for me."

ROANNE ADAMS for BODKIN

Towards the end of 2006, "craving change, freedom, and a way to connect with clients and the end product" Roanne Adams decided to start her own studio in New York. With a strong background in corporate branding, she has been able to transfer this service to her new clients. Understanding the balance between consistent and innovative brand communication, Adams is able to invigorate existing brands with fresh ideas and furnish new companies with the polish of the establishment. "I keep it simple. There is only so much the human mind can digest these days. I think there should be a reason for every aesthetic decision you make. You should be able to back it up and explain why you did what you did, especially when dealing with something as subjective as 'style'."

Fashion has been a consistent obsession for Adams and she draws on this passion in her practice. "I understand the image that fashion designers want to project and how to differentiate them from the slew of other designers." The fashion industry follows a strict schedule, dictated by seasonal catwalk presentations. The pressure of working for a range of brands, all showing collections at the same time, can be intense but with advance planning and support from her studio she thrives on it. "It's a crazy time but totally rewarding," she says.

A new addition to her fashion roster is the sustainable womenswear label Bodkin. Adams is personally dedicated to the challenge of translating the core values of their locally produced, eco-friendly collection into their visual communication. She was appointed art director for the Autumn/Winter 2009/10 catwalk show, she expanded the remit of graphic designer beyond print collateral. Active in the initial planning of the show, she was able to absorb and impart nuanced details to enhance the cohesion of the entire experience. Adams admits that within such a broad context "collaboration plays a huge role. The projects incorporate so many different disciplines. It's all about trust."

The creative process started with a detailed discussion of what inspired the collection: "shapes, cuts, colour palette, fabric choices… and by the end of that conversation I had a bunch of ideas," says Adams. The Horticultural Society of New York was an appropriate location for the show, reinforcing the ethics of the brand and pushing the audience beyond the conventional boundaries of fashion week. The invitations were intended to be useful, interactive and covetable, to take on "multiple uses and encompass a few different layers of ideas". With environmental issues firmly at the heart of the show, air plants were seen as a novel way to reinforce this and also became lasting mementos. The geometric structures of Buckminster Fuller inspired the collection and also the tetrahedron containers for the plants that unfolded into the invitations. Produced with 100 per cent recycled paper and environmentally friendly ink, they also gave instructions for the low-maintenance care of the plants. This is a perfect example of communication working on multiple levels to greatly enhance the depth of the message.

For Adams, the seasonal development and expansion of visual branding is vital for reflecting the progressive nature of the fashion industry. "I think it's important to maintain the core essence of the brand but reinvent it according to a current collection." In direct contrast to the corporate pursuit of mass appeal, Adams notices that her fashion clients demand progressive solutions directed towards niche markets. "The fashion industry is completely image-based, so it gives graphic designers the opportunity to show off, to create things that people don't necessarily have to understand on a literal level." Adams has a unique expertise that allows her to bring her global perspective to burgeoning brands.

www.roanneadams.com
www.bodkinbrooklyn.com

BODKIN →
AUTUMN
WINTER 2009
FEBRUARY 16
4:00-6:00PM
THE HORTICULTURAL
SOCIETY OF NEW YORK
148 W. 37TH STREET,
13TH FLOOR
NEW YORK, NY 10018
BODKINRSVP@PRESS OFFICE.COM
BODKIN IS THE RECIPIENT
OF THE FIRST ECCO DOMANI
SUSTAINABLE DESIGN AWARD

ECCO DOMANI.
WINES OF ITALY

"We chose to have the Bodkin Autumn/ Winter 2009/10 presentation at the Horticultural Society of New York. This location helped dictate the idea of sending out air plants to the attendees. Once that was decided we needed to create an invitation that could serve other purposes besides just inviting people, so we decided to create a container for the plant to be delivered in." The invitation was designed with Cynthia Ratsabouth.

BODKIN →
CARING FOR YOUR AIR PLANTS.
AIR PLANTS, ALSO KNOWN AS TILLANDSIAS, HAVE
NO ROOT SYSTEM. REQUIRE NO SOIL, AND GROW
NON-PARASITICALLY ON THE BRANCHES OF LARGER
TREES. THEY GET ALL THEIR NUTRIENTS FROM THE
DUST AND MOISTURE FOUND IN THE AIR. AIR PLANTS
EASILY ADAPT TO INDOOR CULTURE. GROWN IN THE
WINDOW OR UNDER FLUORESCENT LIGHTS. AVOID
ALL-DAY DIRECT SUNLIGHT. SINCE MOST HOMES
CANNOT MATCH THE MUCH NEEDED HUMIDITY OF
THEIR NATIVE HABITATS, THOROUGHLY SOAK YOUR AIR
PLANT FOR 5 MINUTES, 2-3 TIMES PER WEEK. MORE
OFTEN IN A HOT, DRY ENVIRONMENT; LESS OFTEN IN
A COOL, HUMID ONE. TO PREVENT THE PLANT FROM
ROTTING, SHAKE OUT ANY EXCESS WATER.

SAGMEISTER INC for
ANNI KUAN

Graphic designers work in an industry subject to the fluctuations of personal opinion and regional vernacular, Stefan Sagmeister is one of the very few who has achieved global celebrity status. Intent on making design personal, to touch peoples lives, he creates work that has an emotional connection, but acknowledges that the commercial nature of design can blur this authenticity. Satire, the human body and rebellion are central themes in his work, alongside an intense personal pursuit of honesty; the results are striking and often generate attention.

Originally from Austria, Sagmeister has been based in New York since 1994. His enthusiasm as an educator and lecturer has taken him around the world; travel inspires him and helps to feed his passion for diverse creative dialogue. Undistracted by convention, Sagmeister operates with an objective clarity and foresight. His studio has remained small, allowing him to be selective with clients and creatively liberated because he is financially independent – advice from the late Tibor Kalman. The flexibility this gives him allowed him to close his studio to commercial clients for 12 months in 2001 to focus on creative experimentation. The process was so successful and creatively stimulating that 2009 saw him repeat the adventure.

Sagmeister is realistic about relationships with clients. "It is not possible to do satisfying work for an indifferent client. We need the support and the willingness to collaborate on many levels. They have to want something good." He is unwilling to embrace the restrictions of professional practice and life in general. Mixing business with pleasure was a risky yet logical step when Sagmeister and fashion designer Anni Kuan became a couple in 1998. Eager to impress Kuan, Sagmeister secretly designed a logo and set of business cards, then offered to take on her seasonal invitations. But there was a catch: he would require complete creative control. While their relationship is obviously much closer than that of the average designer and client, rather than collaborate with Kuan, Sagmeister had the confidence to draw on their mutual trust and work independently of any personal or creative complications. Rather than referencing each collection, the goal is to maintain a message that is collectively consistent over the seasons, an arrangement that has been invaluable and ensured the longevity and continued innovation of the invitations. Sagmeister says, "It is very infrequently that Anni will ask for changes in direction."

Like Sagmeister, Kuan limits the size of her studio and business to maintain direct contact with the process of developing a collection. Her label has a broad base of loyal customers and is narrative-driven not trend-based. She originally worked with a minimal budget that only allowed for simple postcard invitations. Sagmeister thought the simplicity was limiting and sought to incorporate more complexity in the message. "It was an invitation and to varying degrees a lookbook of the season," he says. Motivated by an obvious determination to impress, Sagmeister was able to work within the existing financial limitations when a low-cost local newspaper printer was recommended. Since then, the newspaper aesthetic has been an irreplaceable part of the Anni Kuan brand. Rather than being discarded, the invitation has an extended life because of its unique qualities. The natural quality limitations of the printing process

do not reveal the details of the collection yet the invitations function particularly well as reminders.

While each season requires a unique concept, the invitations hold together collectively through the materials used: newsprint, cardboard backing and vacuum packing. In addition, a single element from the concept is exploited; this influences the structure of the invitations, and is folded or physically incorporated in the package. Using a plastic horse or a coat hanger, a bunch of flowers, a folded paper boat or paper crushed into a small ball, Sagmeister reinforces the concept, adding physical depth to the presentation. This is indicative of his intention to explore beyond the conventional two-dimensional restrictions of typography and graphic design in practical ways.

Sagmeister has carved a niche for himself in contemporary design and has inspired a generation of students. Celebrated for his 'rock star' appeal, he is comfortable to be the subject of his designs if this is appropriate. His work for Anni Kuan is a perfect example of his practice of utilizing optical trickery, hand-made typography, the human body and conceptual acrobatics.

www.sagmeister.com
www.annikuan.com

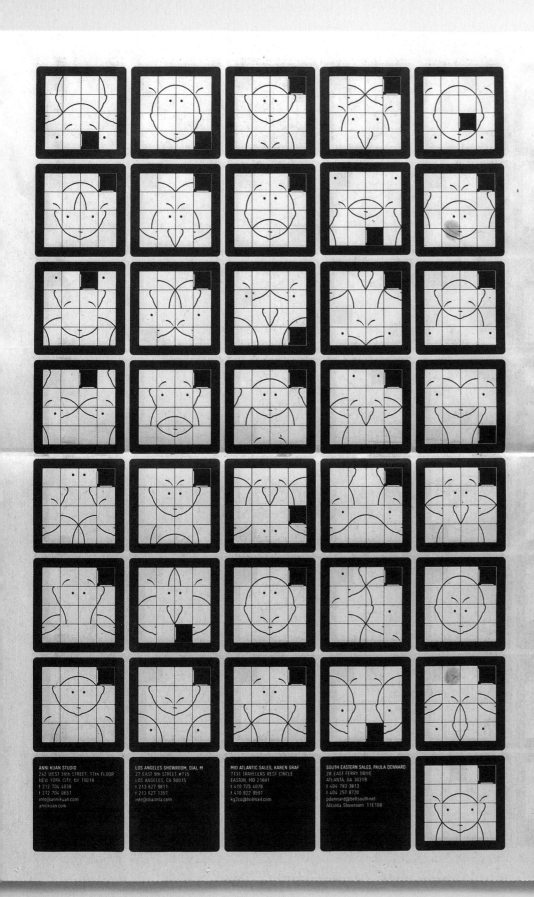

The four-page broadsheet newspaper invitation for Autumn/Winter 2008/09 presents numerous permutations of a classic 4 x 4 slider puzzle, with the original included as a gift. The invitation was designed with Joe Shouldice.

ANNI KUAN STUDIO
242 WEST 38th STREET, 11th FLOOR
NEW YORK CITY, NY 10018
t 212 704 4038
f 212 704 0651
info@annikuan.com
annikuan.com

LOS ANGELES SHOWROOM, DIAL M
27 EAST 9th STREET #715
LOS ANGELES, CA 90015
t 213 627 9811
f 213 627 1357
info@dialmla.com

MID ATLANTIC SALES, KAREN GRAF
7131 TRAVELERS REST CIRCLE
EASTON, MD 21601
t 410 725 4078
f 410 822 9591
kg2co@hotmail.com

SOUTH EASTERN SALES, PAULA DENNARD
28 EAST FERRY DRIVE
ATLANTA, GA 30319
t 404 783 3813
f 404 257 8720
pdennard@bellsouth.net
Atlanta Showroom 11E108

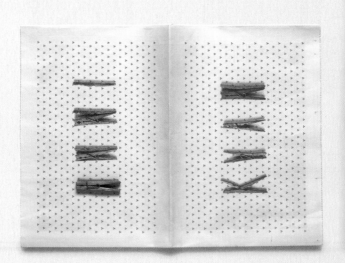

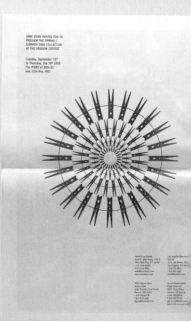

ANNI KUAN INVITES YOU TO
PREVIEW THE SPRING /
SUMMER 2000 COLLECTION
AT THE FASHION COTERIE

Tuesday, September 18th
to Thursday, the 18th 2000
The PIERS at 55th St
and 12th Ave, NYC

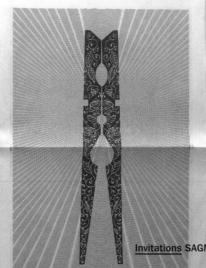

122   Invitations SAGMEISTER INC for ANNI KUAN

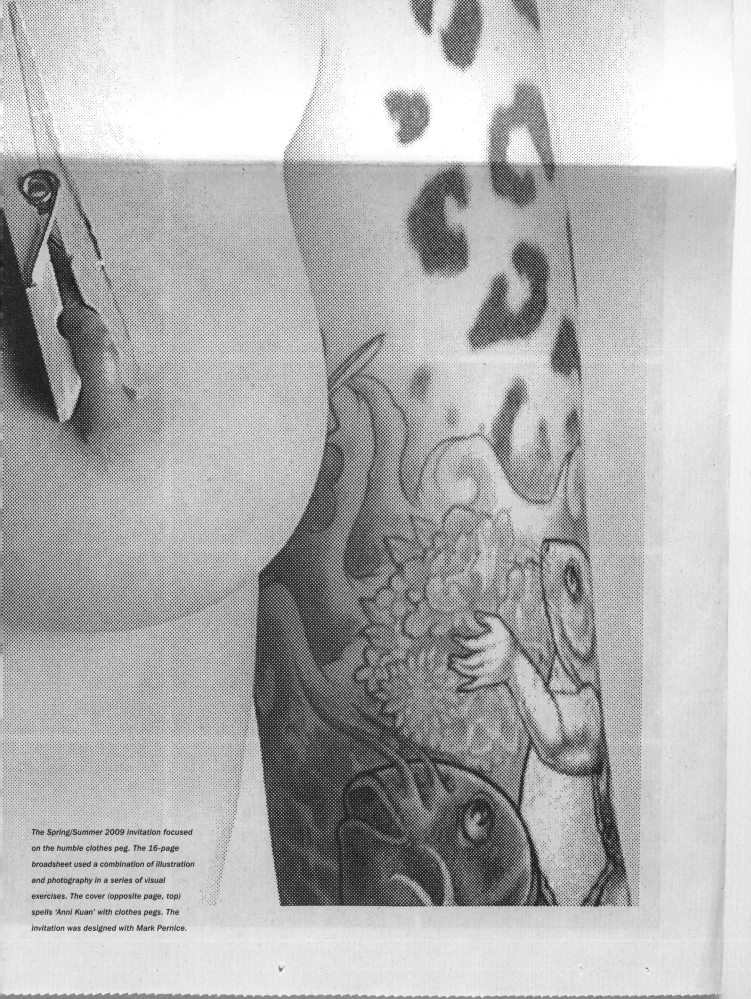

The Spring/Summer 2009 invitation focused on the humble clothes peg. The 16-page broadsheet used a combination of illustration and photography in a series of visual exercises. The cover (opposite page, top) spells 'Anni Kuan' with clothes pegs. The invitation was designed with Mark Pernice.

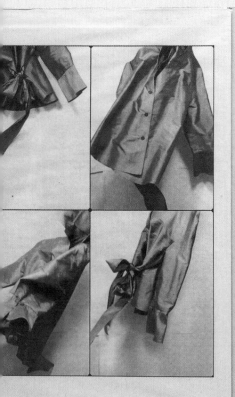

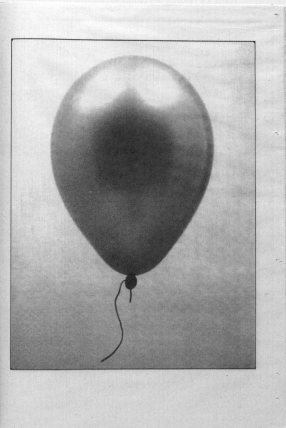

The smaller tabloid formation for Autumn/
Winter 2007/08 ran over 28 pages, featuring
images of Anni Kuan shot inside a photo booth
by Annika Lischke and Quentin Walesch. The
final pages reveal the structure of the set
after it has been dismantled. The back cover
has a strip of photographs with the details
of the collection preview.

*For Spring/Summer 2003 the four-page
broadsheet poster folded into the classic
children's paper hat. The outer side features
typography while the interior includes
images of the collection by Barbara
Gentile. The invitation was designed
with Matthias Ernstberger.*

STUDIO NEWWORK for
ROBERT GELLER

A distinct typographic refinement and enduring sense of sophistication has been central to Studio Newwork's recent rise to prominence. Rigid composition principles underpin dissected letterforms, innovative detailing and creative twists as they refine their visual language. This balance appears instantly timeless, poised between classical and contemporary. *Newwork*, their biannual magazine, has been vital to their development and is extremely well received, encapsulating their aesthetic for potential clients and showcasing their internal creative motivation.

Ryotatsu Tanaka and Ryo Kumazaki began their creative collaboration in 2005 but it was not until 2007, when Hitomi Ishigaki and Aswin Sadha joined them, that Studio Newwork – a phonetic play on New York where they are based – was officially born. A tight-knit studio, looking internally for stimulation and inspiration, their mantra calls for hard work and research. "Study, study, study. More study, better result." Their success within fashion circles is due to their ability to produce covetable pieces of communication that clearly reflect the aspirations of their clients.

Robert Geller has employed the services of Studio Newwork since he started his menswear label in 2006. The collections have a confident romanticism that mixes the masculine with softer elements. The high-quality craftsmanship that goes into the garments is critical for the brand and must be upheld with all print material. Newwork have risen to this challenge with their typographic strength and attention to detail. Without breaking the bank they have infused the complexity in their projects with a perceptive selection of materials that builds contrasting tensions. The results have a polished, genuine accessibility that elevates the message.

Over the seasons the invitations have become a unique conceptual record. While linked by an understated sophistication, each collection has a new direction that the invitations must relate to. Reference sketches, colour swatches and samples are all used as inspiration. The working relationship with Robert Geller is close and Studio Newwork are integrated into the fashion team. This rapport is welcomed by both parties. "Creatively, collaboration always helps us to look at things from a different angle," say Newwork. The trust between studio and client builds creative freedom but they appreciate this freedom requires added responsibility.

The success of the collaboration depends on mutual respect for visual expertise and preferences. "Fashion designers are very careful and sometimes very specific about the choice of colours, fonts and material that create the mood and image of their brand." There seems to be a collective partnership that works to extract the best from each project. With this open platform, differences of opinion are bound to arise, requiring diplomacy and practical explanation. "We are not forceful but are very confident of our vision and what we design, which is always supported by our research."

There is an underlying creative camaraderie to Newwork's philosophy. "People from different creative fields might use different materials to work with but the final goal is the same, which is to deliver messages, ideas and thoughts." Through hard work and trust in their ideas, they believe they can achieve longevity in their work: "We aim to create newness that can last decades." Timelessness is a difficult challenge in the continually evolving fashion industry, yet Newwork seem to have a flair for creating designs for their clients that will continue to feel contemporary.

www.studionewwork.com
www.robertgeller-ny.com

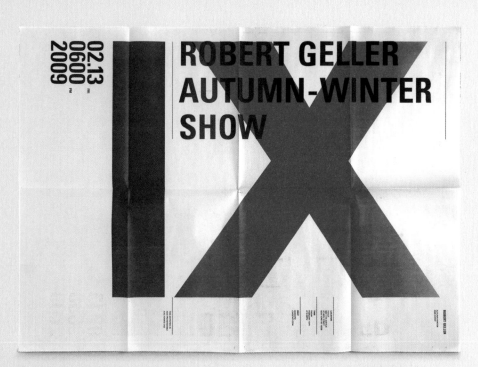

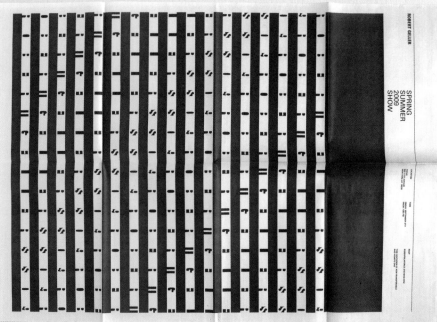

The raw aesthetic of newsprint often features in work by Studio Newwork and for consecutive season invitations it was used for Robert Geller. "For the Autumn/Winter 2009/10 season we designed a new logo for Robert Geller and wanted to use it as the visual element for the invitation. The new logo is a simple black bar so that you see the logo in the design. For example, you see the logo as part of the Roman numeral nine in the design." Stripes were the central element from the Spring/Summer 2009 invitation and were appropriated into the invitation design.

"Inspired by the German art icon, Robert Geller called this his second collection for Spring/Summer 2008 'Beuys Don't Cry'. Robert also mixed his early experience in LA and skateboarding from the 80s with the theme. The fluorescent yellow, trimmed edge of the invitation came from the colour pallete of the collection. The stamp was inspired by actual postcards and letters Joseph Beuys wrote. The key words from the Autumn/Winter 2007/08 collection were 'elegant' and 'classic'. Using UV-coating, shininess creates this great contrast with matt paper to enhance the sense of a classic and elegance."

ROBERT GELLER
NEW YORK

443 WEST 18TH ST
NEW YORK
NY 10011

——

SPRING SUMMER 2008 SHOW

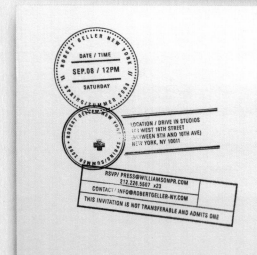

ROBERT GELLER
NEW YORK

AUTUMN / WINTER 2008 SHOW

THIS INVITATION IS NON-TRANSFERABLE
AND ADMITS ONE

RSVP:
PRESS@ROBERTGELLER-NY.COM

DATE / TIME:
FRIDAY FEBRUARY 1ST 2008 / 7:00PM

CONTACT:
INFO@ROBERTGELLER-NY.COM

LOCATION:
ANGEL ORENSANZ FOUNDATION
172 NORFOLK STREET
[BETWEEN HOUSTON ST & STANTON ST]
NEW YORK, NY 10002

"The Autumn/Winter 2008/09 collection was inspired by a book written by an early-nineteenth-century Prussian naturalist. Robert Geller cares about soft material and the quality of washed fabric, the handkerchief represents this part of Robert Geller's clothes as well. The invitations were washed before sending out so they have a nice laundered quality."

STUDIO SMALL for
MARGARET HOWELL

London-based Studio Small approach their practice with simplicity in mind. Founding partners David Hitner and Guy Marshall are focused on the refinement of ideas and not sidetracked by over-analysis. They have been able to build a rational creative process dedicated to their clients' requirements. "We feel it is our role to really listen to the client and communicate their philosophy and personality," says Hitner. A close working relationship is fundamental to ensure results are as pertinent as possible. Small have no house style, and work for a broad range of clients, treating each project as a unique exercise. Their strength lies in their ability to progress and evolve with their clients over time and, as a result, they boast a large number of long-term relationships.

Studio Small began to work for Margaret Howell in 2004, with a commission to design a calendar and poster. The relationship grew and Small went on to replace the in-house design team. While they provided a more objective perspective, Small were tasked with consolidating the existing trust and value in the brand. They embraced the challenge as an exercise to nurture and sensitively develop the brand identity over a range of materials, conscious that stagnation would pose the greatest risk.

The Margaret Howell customer base – primarily architects, designers and professional creatives – is visually discerning and loyal. Beyond the fashion collections and contemporary and vintage furnishings. Margaret Howell also present a wide range of in-store exhibitions that reinforce the central brand aesthetic. From historical to contemporary, the events contribute and build upon the broader interests of Howell and her clientele.

Hitner acknowledges that, "Collaboration is essential. We do not profess to know them or their industry better than they do." Supported by the practical input of Margaret Howell, Small are granted a broad remit to explore creatively. While admitting that a mutual shorthand is advantageous for presenting concepts when working with a creative client, they believe the success of the relationship lies in a shared aesthetic. At the outset of a relationship, it is difficult to evaluate this compatibility, which may not be known until the end of the project. This aesthetic is developed over time and is evident in the increased trust that Small now share with Howell.

In contrast to the consistent reinvention in the broader fashion industry, Margaret Howell collections are a continual progression. Built upon classic tailoring, variations of hue, material and texture timelessly signify the change of season. While a sophisticated message is paramount, the focus on materiality plays to Small's strengths. "It is more about use of materials rather than form," says Hitner. "We are always looking at how to use paper, finishes and combinations of different stock and how it folds down. We try and keep a tactile quality to everything we produce for them because that relates back to who they are in terms of their quality and materials, fabrications and structure."

Self-motivated and determined not to fall into a formula, Small search for a progressive angle to explore each season. Depending on the collection, Howell talk through three or four looks, and perhaps provide only a fabric swatch. The invitations fall into three categories: womenswear, a menswear presentation in Paris and exhibitions throughout the year.

Collectively, the graphic language of the invitations is based on abstracting a key element from a collection. For continuity and distinction, the focus is on fabric and texture for womenswear, menswear is inspired by the construction of the presentation, and invitations to exhibitions are adapted from the subject matter. While directly linked to events, the invitations are successful because they do not reveal details. They are visually striking and the curiosity they arouse can only be resolved by attending a show: receiving one enhances this experience by reinforcing the recipient's anticipation of models walking down the catwalk.

While Small's output is diverse, there is a cohesion to how they communicate the Margaret Howell brand. The invitations represent the first piece of a seasonal puzzle that will later be used in broader supporting material. Small have achieved strength through their consistency, providing Margaret Howell with clear and identifiable visual communication that feels fresh and contemporary.

The men's collection is seasonally presented in Paris as a static exhibition. For the invitations Small use the details of the installation or venue as inspiration. The Spring/Summer 2009 collection presentation was fixed to large wooden boards with punched holes that went on to influence the invitation. "The invitations have relevance to the location but do not give much away about the collection"

www.studiosmall.com
www.margarethowell.co.uk

MARGARET
HOWELL

SS09 MENS PRESENTATION
SUNDAY 29TH JUNE 2008
10:00 – 17:00

108 RUE VIEILLE DU TEMPLE
PARIS 75003

PRESS: MARK FLEMING
+44 (0)20 7009 9003
communications@magarethowell.co.uk

MARGARET
HOWELL

AUTUMN WINTER 09 MENS PRESENTATION

SUNDAY 25TH JANUARY 09
10:00—18:00

MARGARET HOWELL
LA COUR 6 PLACE DE LA MADELEINE 75008 PARIS

PRESS: MARK FLEMING +44 (0)20 7009 9002
COMMUNICATIONS@MARGARETHOWELL.CO.UK

The Autumn/Winter 2009/10 men's
presentation was held at the new
Margaret Howell store. The ceiling
is dotted with skylights that were
used to create an abstract pattern
on the invitation. Traditional material
swatches were used in the Autumn/
Winter 2008/09 presentation and
subsequently scanned in for use
on the invitation.

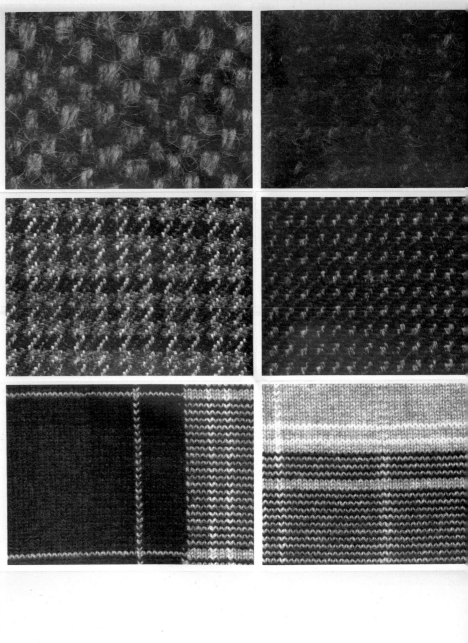

AW08 MENS PRESENTATION
SUNDAY 20TH JANUARY 2008
10:00 – 17:00

108 RUE VIEILLE DU TEMPLE
PARIS 75003

PRESS MARK FLEMING +44 (0)20 7009 9003
COMMUNICATIONS@MARGARETHOWELL.CO.UK
BUYERS JAKE SCOTT +44 (0)20 7009 9018
JAKE@MARGARETHOWELL.CO.UK

MARGARET
HOWELL

Invitations STUDIO SMALL for MARGARET HOWELL

The women's catwalk invitations are directly inspired by the garments. Studio Small meet with Margaret Howell to talk through three or four pieces she considers central to the collection. In some cases all that can be offered for reference is a few material swatches. The women's invitations are more uniform in size, remaining approximately A5. Autumn/Winter 2007/08 was inspired by a pattern and hues from the collection and Spring/Summer 2008 interpreted the polka dot pattern from a piece of fabric from the collection. Only given a single fabric swatch as inspiration for Autumn/Winter 2008/09, Studio Small made it the central feature of the invitation. A graphic abstraction of a scarf was adopted for Autumn/Winter 2009/10.

MARGARET
HOWELL

STUDIO SHOW
AUTUMN WINTER 09
11:00
SATURDAY 21 FEBRUARY
34 WIGMORE STREET
LONDON W1

RSVP SHOW
MODUS PUBLICITY T 00 44 (0)20 7331 1433
PRESS
MARK FLEMING T 00 44 (0)20 7009 9003
communications@margarethowell.co.uk
BUYERS
CHRIS ABBOTT T 00 44 (0)20 7009 9039
chris@margarethowell.co.uk

STUDIO SHOW
SPRING SUMMER 08
MONDAY 17 SEPTEMBER
13:15
34 WIGMORE STREET
LONDON W1

MARGARET
HOWELL

RSVP SHOW
MODUS PUBLICITY T 00 44 (0)20 7331 1433
PRESS
MARK FLEMING T 00 44 (0)20 7009 9003
communications@margarethowell.co.uk
BUYERS
CHRIS ABBOTT T 00 44 (0)20 7009 9039
chris@margarethowell.co.uk

MARGARET
HOWELL

MARGARET
HOWELL

STUDIO SHOW
AUTUMN WINTER 08
13:15
THURSDAY 14 FEBRUARY
34 WIGMORE STREET
LONDON W1

RSVP SHOW
MODUS PUBLICITY T 00 44 (0)20 7331 1433
PRESS
MARK FLEMING T 00 44 (0)20 7009 9003
communications@margarethowell.co.uk
BUYERS
CHRIS ABBOTT T 00 44 (0)20 7009 9039
chris@margarethowell.co.uk

MARGARET
HOWELL

STUDIO SHOW
AUTUMN WINTER 07
13:45
THURSDAY 15 FEBRUARY
34 WIGMORE STREET
LONDON W1

RSVP SHOW
MODUS PUBLICITY T 00 44 (0)20 7331 1433
PRESS
MARK FLEMING T 00 44 (0)20 7009 9003
communications@margarethowell.co.uk
BUYERS
CHRIS ABBOTT T 00 44 (0)20 7009 9039
chris@margarethowell.co.uk

MARGARET
HOWELL

For Spring/Summer 2009 bars of black flocking again referenced garments from the collection. "We keep looking at how we can use Gill Sans in a slightly different way, the thing about Gill Sans, if you are not careful it can look very retro and very 60's, it is about keeping it looking very modern."

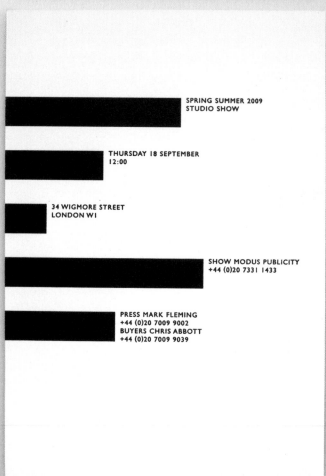

SPRING SUMMER 2009
STUDIO SHOW

THURSDAY 18 SEPTEMBER
12:00

34 WIGMORE STREET
LONDON W1

SHOW MODUS PUBLICITY
+44 (0)20 7331 1433

PRESS MARK FLEMING
+44 (0)20 7009 9002
BUYERS CHRIS ABBOTT
+44 (0)20 7009 9039

A colour palette and grid system inspired by the Bauhaus movement, was applied to a poster for the Spring/Summer 2007 invitation.

MARGARET
HOWELL

SS07
MENS PRESENTATION
SUNDAY 2 JULY 2006
10:00 TO 18:00

GALERIE XAVIER SEQUIER
10 RUE DU BOURG L'ABBÉ
PARIS 75003

PRESS: MARK FLEMING +44 (0)20 7009 9003
COMMUNICATIONS@MARGARETHOWELL.CO.UK

STUDIOTHOMSON for PREEN

For brothers Christopher and Mark Thomson, with their independent backgrounds in prominent design studios, it was a tentative yet logical step for them to cast aside any thoughts of sibling rivalry and form StudioThomson in 2005. The practice is based on an almost tangible mutual trust, and while it is undoubtedly a close-knit operation, surprisingly they do not share an office. Instead they have opted for home studios on opposite sides of London. Regular meetings, with each other and collaborators, are intentionally scheduled to create time away from the computer: now that they have creative freedom and independence they do not want to be tied to the machine. Their ability to work separately while producing a consistent body of work is proof of their aesthetic clarity. They are not swayed by trends, preferring to focus on content and ensure their work remains desirable into the future.

Before the launch of StudioThomson, Mark Thomson had been introduced to Preen by mutual friends and was commissioned to design the label's Spring/Summer 2004 invitations. He was attracted to the project by the intricacy in the detailing of the collection and the opportunity to stretch his creativity in what was then a side project to his regular job. A little over a year later StudioThomson were formed, with Preen as one of the original clients. They remain central to the studio; both parties have grown together over the years and enjoy each other's company. Christopher and Mark Thomson seem to seek out clients with whom they can build long-term, mutually productive partnerships, similar to their own internal relationship. They consider their creative process a collective experience with Preen, not necessarily a collaboration. As a practical form of quality control, Preen are kept abreast of their progress throughout a project to ensure that any problems that develop are resolved at the earliest possible moment.

This continual dialogue is vital to the relationship between StudioThomson and Preen. Invitations for an upcoming collection are discussed at Preen's studio, with the help of moodboards and maybe some rough photographs of garments. It is an open discussion: "Preen do not dictate what they want. We discuss the collection and then go away to get on with it. They respect what we do and encourage us to be creative with it," says Mark Thomson. The concepts of Preen's very eclectic seasonal influences set their creative framework. StudioThomson interpret it, from gig tickets to childlike oversized proportions, and are careful to ensure the invitations are relevant, yet only offer a hint of what is to come. "Preen don't want to give away too much, it has to be quite subtle."

For StudioThomson, invitations provide the perfect opportunity to experiment with new techniques and processes, as volumes are relatively low and creative expectations are high. Materials, textures and finishes are selected with care to enhance the overall concept. For Autumn/Winter 2004/05 Preen contrasted their established deconstructive aesthetic with a distinct air of sophistication. StudioThomson captured this duality with opposing sides to the invitation: the front was clean, white and timeless, and was juxtaposed with an uncoated, raw texture and rubber stamp type on the reverse. This successful balance provided an intuitive link to the collection without directly revealing any details.

StudioThomson are highly self-motivated in their search for new ideas and challenges. This is in part due to their dedication to their clients but is also indicative of their personal pursuit of satisfaction in the work they do. They seem to be inspired by everything other than graphic design, regular visits to exhibitions and museums are a central form of research and source of inspiration. Their practice has a positive attitude that comes from the freedom they enjoy in their profession and their lifestyle. They are not restricted by the world of graphic design and this is clearly translated into their final products.

www.studiothomson.com
www.preen.eu

PREEN BY THORNTON BREGAZZI
AUTUMN WINTER 2004/5

Preen by Thornton Bregazzi
Spring Summer 2010

Friday September 11 at 12pm
Milk Studios, 2nd Floor Gallery
450 W. 15th Street
New York NY 10011

RSVP
preen@bpcm.com

TUESDAY 17TH FEBRUARy AT 12.00 PM

EMPRESS STATE BUILDING, 55 LILLIE ROAD

LONDON SW6 1TR (NEAREST TUBE – WEST BROMPTON)

NAME _____ SEAT ____

RSVP: mark@concretelondon.com

TEL: +44(0)20 7434 4333

FAX: +44(0)20 7434 4555

TOPSHOP   GenerationPress

"There were two sides to the Autumn/Winter
2004/05 collection. A very sophisticated
side was contrasted with a more grungy
side and Preen were mixing the two
elements. We produced a two-sided
invitation with one side foiled and quite
sophisticated and the other more lo-fi to
represent the other aspect of it. The thick
black lines on this Spring/Summer 2010
invitation were inspired by the way bondage
ropes are tied on the body, which was a
theme running through this collection. There
was also a lot of see-through mesh material
used in the garments, so we photographed
various bits of the material to look like they
were on bodies, and applied them to the
shapes created by the thick black lines.
We used a thin bible paper for the invite
and printed on both sides to continue
the transparent theme of the collection."

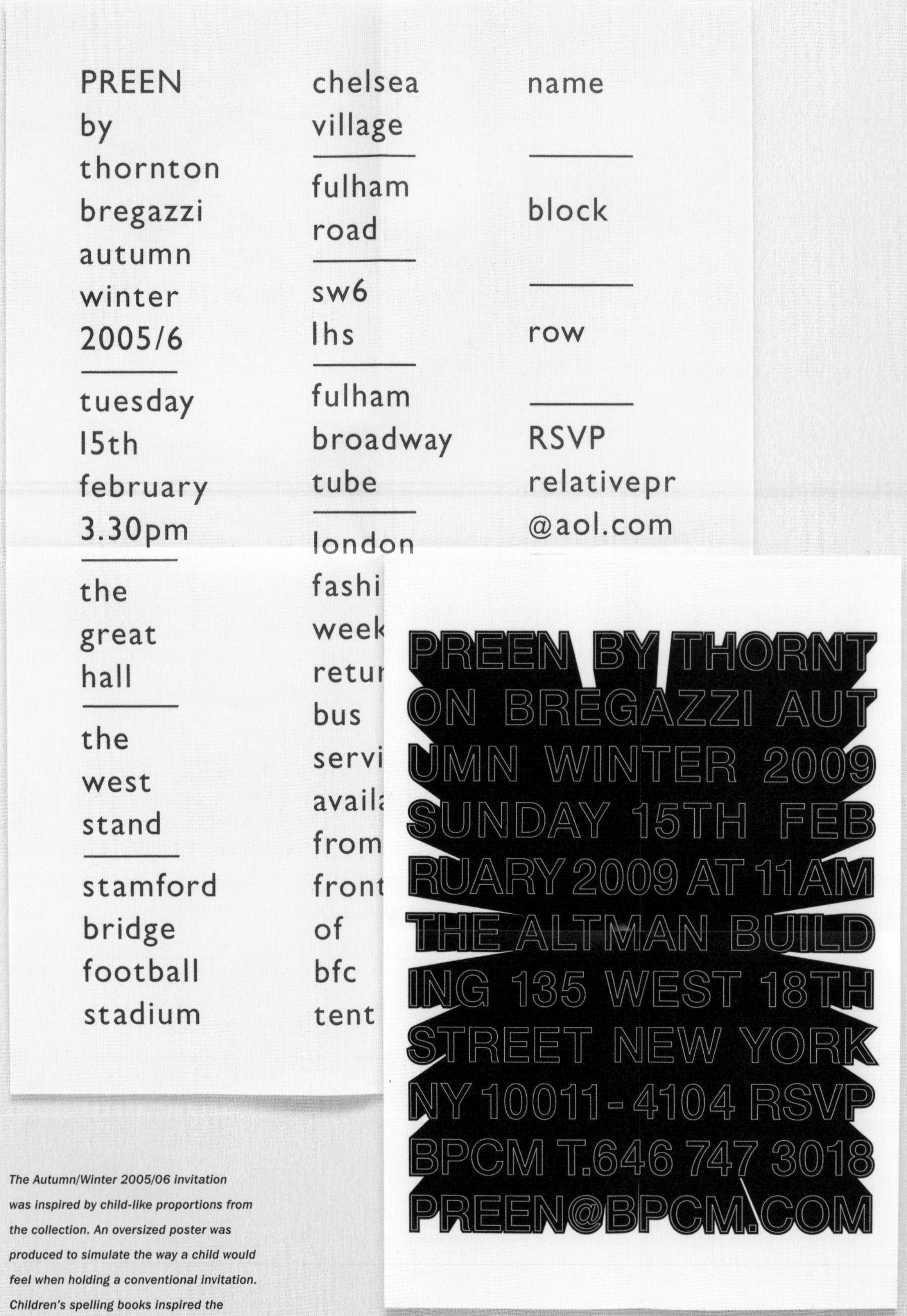

PREEN
by
thornton
bregazzi
autumn
winter
2005/6

tuesday
15th
february
3.30pm

the
great
hall

the
west
stand

stamford
bridge
football
stadium

chelsea
village

fulham
road

sw6
lhs

fulham
broadway
tube

london
fashi
week
retur
bus
servi
availa
from
front
of
bfc
tent

name

block

row

RSVP
relativepr
@aol.com

PREEN BY THORNT ON BREGAZZI AUT UMN WINTER 2009 SUNDAY 15TH FEB RUARY 2009 AT 11AM THE ALTMAN BUILD ING 135 WEST 18TH STREET NEW YORK NY 10011-4104 RSVP BPCM T.646 747 3018 PREEN@BPCM.COM

The Autumn/Winter 2005/06 invitation was inspired by child-like proportions from the collection. An oversized poster was produced to simulate the way a child would feel when holding a conventional invitation. Children's spelling books inspired the typography. Preen were the source of inspiration for Autumn/Winter 2009/10. It was a particularly space age collection and this directly influenced the typography.

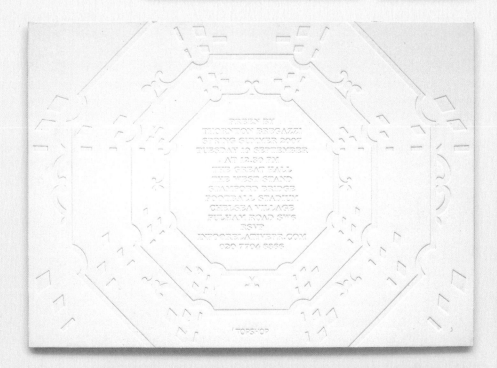

PREEN BY
THORNTON BREGAZZI
SPRING SUMMER 2009
SUNDAY 7 SEPTEMBER AT 2PM
ESPACE, 635 WEST 42ND ST
NEW YORK NY 10036
RSVP - BPCM
T 646 747 3018
E PREEN@BPCM.COM

TOPSHOP
M·A·C   SWAROVSKI   AVEDA

NAME

. . . .

. . . .

SEAT . . . .

ROW . . . .

PREEN
BY
THORNTON BREGAZZI

A constant point of reference for all Preen collections, music was a particular focal point for Spring/Summer 2009, which translated into creating a gig ticket for the invitation. Band posters from the 1970s were the inspiration with loads of band logos and different fonts all together. "At the entrance to the show they actually tore one side off as you would when going into a gig." Two prominent themes of the Spring/Summer 2007 collection were the film 2001: A Space Odyssey and ornate furniture associated with the reign of Louise XIV. "We created a white, debossed invite to give it a space-age feel, with graphics representing the interior of a spaceship, but with seventeenth-century details integrated into it that you would normally find on furniture of that period. The typeface was also intended to be a nod to the period of Louis XIV." The music theme was again influential for Autumn/Winter 2008/09. There was a grunge element to the collection that resulted in the invitations referencing the typography of the pivotal Nirvana album Nevermind.

PREEN BY
THORNTON BREGAZZI
AUTUMN WINTER 2008
SUNDAY 3 FEBRUARY AT 2PM
ESPACE, 635 WEST 42ND ST
NEW YORK, NY 10036
RSVP-BPCM
T 646 747 3018
E PREEN@BPCM.COM
SEAT___ROW___

PREEN
BY
THORNTON BREGAZZI

TOPSHOP

SWAROVSKI

M·A·C

Bumble and bumble.

THORBJØRN ANKERSTJERNE for
BLAAK

The London-based designer Thorbjørn Ankerstjerne is tireless in his pursuit of new challenges and innovative solutions. In an effort to leave the printed page behind, he reinvents his process with every project in order to push beyond the conventional materials of graphic design and create unexpected results. "I don't have a favourite typeface. I would not want to repeat myself by establishing a particular style. I don't want to pursue one direction," he says. This is not an act of defiance; rather it is a way to broaden the area from which he can draw inspiration and explore concepts. Such an approach is most successful when he is actively supported by a client.

This is particularly evident in Ankerstjerne's relationship with the London menswear label Blaak, with whom he has worked since 2008. He acknowledges that a shared creative language is a particular advantage in their collaboration as both parties are driven to create visually innovative solutions. "Working with creatives, you are in the same team. I can talk with Blaak about the hue, smell and touch of paper, not just the cost implications." It is a mutually beneficial relationship as Ankerstjerne is exposed to Blaak's experience and decision-making, which is valuable for his own practice.

Designing graphic material in advance of a completed collection is common in the fashion industry, particularly for invitations. Ankerstjerne intentionally draws Blaak directly into his creative process by supplying an extended range of possible solutions. The discussion of these initial ideas provides a tangible insight into which of them are most appropriate. The subsequent editing and refinement ensure greater understanding of the goals and that the most appropriate solution is recognized. "That is

why I really like to work with other people – because it is not my idea, but it grows, you push each other into something better and more exciting than what you started out with. That is why it is important to have a good relationship, so you can question the progress honestly."

Although Ankerstjerne works for a wide range of clients, he relishes the unique challenges provided by Blaak. "The pace and fast rhythm of the fashion industry is very inspiring. It's a challenge to see if you can come up with something that can represent that." He sees designing for fashion as being like a boxing match with ideas, competing within a limited time-frame. "It is a creative exercise of idea versus idea." With much determination and effort, the strongest idea is left standing. Rather than resulting in a compromise that dilutes the end result, this approach is a way of filtering Ankerstjerne's wealth of ideas and discovering solutions that are both innovative and appropriate for Blaak.

Ankerstjerne feels that the creativity fashion designers invest in a brand is a major factor in their interest in the graphic design that supports it. "Blaak feel so strongly about their designs that they cannot help but get involved." Differences of opinion are bound to arise but Ankerstjerne insists he is not dogmatic. He believes the collaborative process results in a mutual respect that provides a solid base from which to move beyond differences and find a solution that everyone is not only happy with, but which also excites them.

While it is clear Ankerstjerne has great passion for his work, his ability to personalize and democratize the creative process enables him to enjoy an intimate working relationship with clients. "I see clients more as people

or individuals. I am open-minded and do not have a certain way of doing things. I also like it when clients inspire me." Perhaps most importantly, his focus is on a mutually beneficial relationship, which transforms the labour of graphic design from a profession into a pleasure.

www.ankerstjerne.co.uk
www.blaak.co.uk

Selection of Spring/Summer 2009 invitations. "The main concept was to show the feeling of the collection that was about an 'adventurous travelling man with mud on his boots.' We wanted to create an intimate and personal invitation for people to keep afterwards."

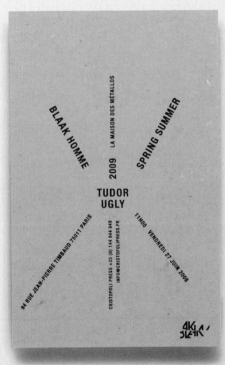

Invitations THORBJØRN ANKERSTJERNE for BLAAK

MAN
VS
MACHINE
BLAAK HOMME
AUTUMN WINTER 2009
11H00 VENDREDI
23 JANVIER 2009
DOOR STUDIOS
9-9 BIS RUE
LESDIGUIÈRES 75004 PARIS
RSVP CRISTOFOLI PRESS
+33 (0) 1 44 84 49 49
INFO@CRISTOFOLIPRESS.FR

The Autumn/Winter 2009/10
'Man vs Machine' catwalk invitation
was produced by hand in the studio.

LOOKBOOKS

ARE A VISUAL DOCUMENTATION OF A SINGLE SEASON. EXCLUSIVELY DISTRIBUTED TO MEMBERS OF THE FASHION INDUSTRY, LOOKBOOKS BECOME A PHYSICAL ARCHIVE OF THE FASHION LABEL.

INTRODUCTION

WHETHER A PURELY FUNCTIONAL VEHICLE OF CATWALK IMAGES ENCLOSED BY A LOGO-EMBLAZONED COVER OR A CONCEPTUAL EXTENSION OF THE COLLECTION, THE LOOKBOOK IS FIRST AND FOREMOST A PRACTICAL TOOL. HIGHLY COVETABLE AND WITH LIMITED DISTRIBUTION, THE SEASONAL BOOKLETS ARE FREE AND FEEL MORE LIKE A PERSONAL GIFT. NOT AVAILABLE TO THE GENERAL PUBLIC, THE LOOKBOOK SPEAKS TO A SELECT GROUP OF PRESS, STYLISTS, BUYERS AND PHOTOGRAPHERS INSIDE THE FASHION INDUSTRY. WITH A TARGET AUDIENCE OF SUCH COLLECTIVE CREATIVE AWARENESS, THE EXPECTATIONS FOR THE GRAPHIC DESIGNER ARE HIGH.

RECENT TECHNOLOGY NOW FACILITATES ALMOST IMMEDIATE TRANSFER OF IMAGES DIRECTLY FROM THE CATWALK TO THE INTERNET. WITH THIS INSTANT DISTRIBUTION IN CONJUNCTION WITH DIGITAL ARCHIVING, THE BASIC FUNCTION OF LOOKBOOKS HAS BEEN CHALLENGED. RATHER THAN MARGINALIZE THE PRACTICE, IT HAS GENERATED EVER MORE INNOVATIVE CREATIVE RESPONSES THAT EXTEND THE CATWALK EXPERIENCE.

HOW DO YOU KNOW WHEN SOMETHING IS GOOD? IF I CAN STRONGLY SENSE ITS PRESENCE[150] IT'S ALL IN THE STOMACH REALLY… OR LET'S PUT IT THE OTHER WAY AROUND – IT FEELS TERRIBLE WHEN SOMETHING IS BAD…[152] THAT'S AN INTUITIVE THING. UNFORTUNATELY THERE ARE NO ABSOLUTE CRITERIA[158] IT WORKS. IT FEELS RIGHT[164] WHEN THERE IS NO EASY POINT OF IMPROVEMENT. EVERYTHING IS VERY CLEAR BUT HARD TO PUT INTO WORDS WHY OR HOW. YOU CAN FEEL SOME SORT OF INTENSE COMPLEXITY BUT IT'S HARD TO VERBALIZE THE BUILDING BLOCKS[170] SOMETHING COULD BE GOOD FOR ME OR CHALLENGING, BUT THAT DOES NOT MEAN IT WILL BE CONSIDERED GOOD FOR EVERYONE[178] THE ONLY WAY IS TO BELIEVE IN YOUR VISUAL SENSE[188] IF THE CLIENT LIKES IT FOR THE SAME REASONS AS WE DO[200] WE ARE TWO DIFFERENT CHARACTERS AND WE BOTH NEED TO AGREE THAT THE WORK IS GOOD[204] WHEN YOU DON'T WANT TO CHANGE ANYTHING[208] WHEN I MAKE SOMETHING, I ALWAYS SEE JUST FORM AND VALUE OF ELEMENTS. IF I CAN FEEL SOMETHING POETIC IN MY COMPOSITION, I CAN SAY THIS IS BETTER[212] IT'S DIFFICULT TO EXPRESS WHAT MAKES A PROJECT 'GOOD' IN ABSTRACT TERMS. I AM PERSONALLY MOVED BY WORK THAT IS SERIOUS, UNWASTEFUL, MODERN (IN CONCEPTION), SENSUOUS, UNPRETENTIOUS, ENGAGING AND REFINED[216]

BLUEMARK INC for SALLY SCOTT

Bluemark blur the line between the artistic and the commercial. Atsuki Kikuchi, the studio's art director and founding partner, has a background in fine art and clearly brings this sensitivity into his work. The decision to move into graphic design was in part a result of it being integrated with other disciplines. Kikuchi does not want to be isolated by practising only one speciality, and sees graphic design as a creative mediator that facilitates commissioned and self-initiated projects through its many applications, with no restrictions to limit his interest and imagination.

Beyond the conventional applications of a design studio, Bluemark support a diverse range of interconnected creative and commercial activities. They operate cafés, galleries and even a recording studio that run parallel with their graphic design clients, all supported by Bluemark design, publishing and distribution channels. This facilitates the supply and demand of Bluemark's creative know-how and provides an alternative framework for ideas and products.

Kikuchi defines design as "a structural way of thinking. Depending on the brand I'm working for I try to adapt a different personality, almost like an actor, in order to get into the right mood for the project." He mentally distils a project into the basic components of communication and, from this common ground, is able to build a new experience with greater clarity and efficiency. It is his adopted persona or unique perspective that develops the creative response. For this reason he is indifferent as to whether he shares a creative language with his clients. "Respect is more important than understanding. As long as we respect each other's work we don't necessarily have to understand each other."

There is a quirky innocence to the work and practice of Bluemark that is particularly suited to the subtle, narrative-based designs of Sally Scott, which are often based around a single character. With a long-term relationship that stretches back to 2002, Bluemark have been responsible for the development of the label's complete visual language. The logo was inspired by a second-hand children's book and adds personality to the brand. "The fact that it's not just a name and an address, but also reveals something of the personality behind fascinated me. There is already a lot of narrative in the logotype," says Kikuchi.

This is reaffirmed in the Sally Scott lookbooks as they too reference the narrative, structure and materials of children's books. "I begin with taking a close look at a new collection and trying to think myself into it. When the shooting is done, I do my best to make everything fit together into a harmonious overall picture. The colour of the cover is a result of earlier decisions like location, mood and styling."

Consistency and collective appeal have always been at the heart of the lookbooks, which also utilize the seasonal nature of fashion. Kikuchi admits, "Long-term planning makes the design much more difficult because you still have to like what you created years before." The commitment to an established format has allowed greater attention and effort to be directed towards the seasonal concept and its execution. The Sally Scott website provides specific details of garments, allowing the lookbook to function as an independent visual exercise that creatively interprets the mood of a collection. Working with the same photography team has also enhanced the creative effect. Rather than being a reinvention, each lookbook is part of a building process that enhances the bigger story of Sally Scott. "The relationship is of course very smooth, because we know and trust each other completely," says Kikuchi.

Bluemark are pioneers in the fight against a wave of homogenous design. The designers pursue a creative intimacy in their work, and this in turn results in greater appreciation and respect from clients. Their mutual confidence and the diversity of their work ensures that their motivation remains high and that they are emotionally involved in their projects.

"I begin with taking a close look at a new collection and trying to think myself into it. When the shooting is done I do my best to make everything fit together into a harmonious overall picture. The colour of the cover is a result of earlier decisions like location, mood and styling." The consistent format of 21 x 14cm (8¼ x 14in) and cloth hardcover has contributed to the collectability of the lookbooks. Printing direction was supplied by Takashi Ochiai (Graph).

www.bluemark.co.jp
www.sallyscott.com

DESIGNBOLAGET for WON HUNDRED

In pursuit of a more progressive and personally satisfying creative practice, in 2002 Claus Due decided to establish his own studio. Based in Copenhagen, its name – Designbolaget – translates as 'design company' and is a play on that of Sweden's state-operated alcohol retailer Systembolaget ('system company'). With previous experience in advertising, Due wanted to refocus his attention on graphic design as the central component of his creative process. Although he works predominantly in print, he operates across a wide remit of art, music and fashion projects to satisfy his diverse interests. With a keen sense of wit and creative enthusiasm, Designbolaget strike the perfect balance between function and concept.

The Scandinavian fashion industry is strong but, apart from a few major exceptions, it is relatively insular. In direct contrast to the stereotypical statuesque, lacquered aesthetic, Designbolaget produce work that has a natural clarity and honesty. Without the gloss, there is an ease to the message; it has an accessibility that is balanced with aspiration. "When you work with fashion clients it is much more about intuition and good taste, you can feel if it is right. There is a shared language. It is OK to talk about feelings and whether something is nice or not nice," says Due. He acknowledges that the larger financial investment associated with advertising means 'feelings' are not enough; there has to be a quantifiable strategy, which leaves little room for the risk-taking required for creative innovation.

Won Hundred is a men's and women's fashion line that produces seasonal collections supported by an extensive range of basics. Subtle themes run through the designs for each collection, leaving room for personal creative interpretation. It was launched in 2004 and Designbolaget were called in three years later. Typical of the relative close quarters of the Copenhagen creative industry, both studio and client are on the same street. This physical proximity strengthens the relationship between them and a close rapport has developed.

Designbolaget are responsible for the full range of Won Hundred's print material, and in the absence of a regular catwalk presentation the lookbooks have an added importance in communicating the company's direction each season. The creative dynamic of producing them is enhanced by Femmes Regionales, who collaborate on the art direction and style the photography. While Won Hundred are involved throughout the production of the books, they do not participate directly in the creative process, entrusting Designbolaget and Femmes Regionales to drive the project forward. "They are sharp clients, they are really focused but they rely on us as well."

Embracing the responsibility of this freedom, Due approached the Spring/Summer 2008 collection looking for a way to extend the basic concept of the lookbook. This produced the idea of working with 100 pieces of clothing that ran across 100 pages. The end result extended the branding of the label beyond the name or logo, and provided a solid platform from which to build in the future. At times images bled off the page to be completed overleaf, creating a seamless connection from one page to the next. The luxury of so many pages was not wasted: an endless stream of visual exercises and paper stock variations made readers eager to turn them. The book's success undoubtedly attracted a lot of attention to the brand, and repaid the trust Won Hundred placed in the creative team. Over the last two seasons the company's lookbooks have evolved into more commercially driven publications, while retaining their core aesthetic. From 100 pages in 2008 to the Spring/Summer 2009 lookbook which featured 100 likes and dislikes, Designbolaget have maintained consistency while ensuring that their client's changing requirements continue to be met.

Designbolaget are very thorough in how they react to a brief, which means they are able to justify, and if necessary defend, their ideas. "We are good at listening to what the clients have to say. That is a really big part of our job and contribution. I think that is why the small studios are doing well, we meet the people and we talk to the people and we can sense them. We can sense each other's aesthetic." Due's direct involvement in every project undoubtedly reassures his clients, as his dedication to pursuing innovative solutions is clear to see.

www.designbolaget.dk
www.wonhundred.com

The second lookbook by Designbolaget for the Autumn/Winter 2008/09 season advanced the aesthetic from the previous issue while maintaining the same format. The flatplan cover was photographed on the studio wall – with a special guest – to indicate a change of direction to a more analogue design aesthetic. The photographer Sacha Maric was commissioned to bring a more physical quality to the images and has continued to collaborate on all following lookbooks. "I have to feel something when I am looking at the pictures. Sasha has put something human into these pictures, it does not have that distance."

Lookbooks DESIGNBOLAGET for WON HUNDRED

At 22 x 29.5cm (8½ x 11½in) and 100 pages, the Spring/Summer 2008 lookbook also uses multiple paper stocks and feels more like a fashion magazine. In collaboration with Femmes Regionales and with photography by Asger Carlsen the title flows through a range of photostories with additional poetry by M.C. Jabber. Designbolaget pulled all these components together to create a cohesive message. "The images were in every direction, there was no style, black and white, colour, studio, outside. So we decided to use 100 pages to try and find something that would tie it all together. It became obvious that the cover would have to show all 100 pages and we completed the design in two days over the weekend."

THE FOLLOWING
STATEMENT IS TRUE

While the Autumn/Winter 2009/10 lookbook maintained the 100 pages, the format was reduced to 17 x 24cm (6½ x 9½in). Subtle, photocopied typography supported the analogue aesthetic established in the previous issue, while the photography became more direct and functional. "From my background I am thinking about the branding and identity. I try to make the client recognisable from one season to the next."

Lookbooks **DESIGNBOLAGET for WON HUNDRED**

Hate, being put on hold ...

The pagination was reduced by half for
Spring/Summer 2009 and 'The Book of
LOVE, HATE and Everything in Between.'
To maintain the central concept of 100
the lookbook carried 100 examples
of love and hate that were interwoven
with studio and location photography.

FREUDENTHAL VERHAGEN for BERNHARD WILLHELM

Carmen Freudenthal and Elle Verhagen joined forces immediately after college in 1988, and since then they have earned an international reputation for their unique visual fantasies. Based in Amsterdam, the duo build rich, surrealist visions layered on detailed conceptual narratives. Inspired by both the classic and the contemporary, their work has a polish that blurs the line between reality and fiction and creates tension. They are creative innovators whose products are consistently infused with a sharp wit that, again, puts viewers off-balance. "First of all it should of course make sense, but just as important, it should be something new and if possible, please let it be funny (in an unexpected way)," says Freudenthal.

Although fashion was always an important part of their work, Freudenthal and Verhagen were increasingly inspired by the Dutch scene in the late 1990s and made a conscious decision to concentrate on fashion editorials. Primarily a photography and styling team, without any experience in graphic design, they were more than surprised when Bernhard Willhelm commissioned them to produce a complete lookbook. While they grew more confident about the potential of graphic design with each season, it was used exclusively to enhance the imagery. "The first lookbooks we made for Bernhard Willhelm were just a collection of photographs with a staple to hold them together. After a couple of lookbooks we started thinking about layout and typography to enrich the visuals," Freudenthal says.

A successful and mutually satisfying relationship with Willhelm evolved that covered lookbooks from 2001 to 2007. Willhelm is well known to offer his collaborators creative freedom, completely trusting in their ability and experience. Freudenthal believes this is common within the fashion industry. "We get more freedom to make a personal translation of the product with our fashion clients. They want added value from us. The collaboration is therefore more in the field of inspiration and less in controlling the final message." The duo look for clients who facilitate their ideas, rather than ones who collaborate actively with them.

Willhelm encouraged Freudenthal and Verhagen to 'interpret' his collections, and produce print-based extensions of his garments. Bringing together historical, ethnic and pop culture influences each season is an independent exercise that requires an original lookbook solution. As such, each collection has inspired an increasingly elaborate and varied visual response, from computer games to ghosts, from collage to advanced image manipulation. Freudenthal and Verhagen are extremely self-motivated and thrive on having collective responsibility for a project, from concept to photography to graphic design. "The unique thing in all the Bernhard Willhelm lookbooks when you compare them to other products is we had the total freedom to do as we liked and were in control of the overall look," says Verhagen.

With this freedom, it is important to start with background information before the creative process begins. "It's a back and forth process: think about the boundaries to have a focus, then try to forget about the boundaries to give unexpected ideas a chance," says Freudenthal. This can be difficult with fashion, as garments often do not arrive until the day of the shoot. Willhelm talks Freudenthal and Verhagen through the collection as a conceptual abstraction and from this they build a flexible structure on which to focus their energy. Sheer lack of time means adaptability is vital.

Although the relationship with Willhelm has been fruitful and supportive, Freudenthal does not see a shared creative background as a prerequisite. "I don't like to generalize. A client from a non-creative background can be just as understanding." This perhaps reflects the fact that she and Verhagen operate comfortably without a great deal of client involvement; mutual respect is the key element. However, as a duo and often as leaders of larger teams, collaboration is fundamental to their process. "Everything is 200 per cent teamwork. Between the two of us, but also with other collaborators on a specific project," says Freudenthal. In the increasingly homogenized world of fashion, Freudenthal Verhagen continue to forge their own path, maintaining their independent spirit and visual style.

www.freudenthalverhagen.com
www.totemfashion.com

For Spring/Summer 2006 the lookbook was produced as two A1 posters. "This was the superwoman collection. Before the shoot we had the idea to show Bernhard and Jutta as giants being attacked by their own creations, mean little fashion elves," says Verhagen. "The day before the show the collection arrived and (as usual) everything had to be shot in one day in Bernhard's studio in Paris," says Freudenthal.

OF COURSE

"The Autumn/Winter 2002/03 lookbook represented a conscious effort to include more graphic design in our work. We shot the supporting images in and around Amsterdam and 'collaged' them together with the main looks to make it feel like it was all done in Paris. We also asked Chris Pugmire and Sharon Cleary to add text to the comic book. The goal was to bring a liberal, Provo feel to the lookbook."

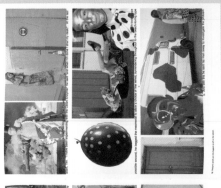

nly to fan anger but also to raise eyebrows among critics who say his regional policy has lacked clarity

WOW

BERNHARD WILLHELM SPRING/SUMMER 2003
LOOKBOOK BY CARMEN FREUDENTHAL & ELLE VERHAGEN

"The central themes for the Spring/Summer 2003 were do-it-yourself, construction and flowers. We shot on location at a building site in the middle of the flower bulb region of the Netherlands. The Dutch 'Floriade' is an international exhibition of flowers and gardens that is only held once every ten years. The event was taking place nearby so we were able to incorporate shots from there, in particular the cover image."

Lookbooks FREUDENTHAL VERHAGEN for **BERNHARD WILLHELM**

"We made the Spring/Summer 2007 lookbook right after the show in our studio in Amsterdam. Bernhard used very young models in his show and wanted to do something about computers for the lookbook. That was our starting point," says Freudenthal.

HARRIMANSTEEL for
ELEY KISHIMOTO

Intent on finding a way to use their diverse creativity, college friends Julian Harriman-Dickinson and Nick Steel opened HarrimanSteel in 1999. They are able to move between advertising and design, print and moving image with relative ease, as their primary focus is on creative communication and engagement with the audience. This breadth of interest is maintained by constant visual awareness. "Keep your eyes open, watch and listen. Be inspired by the things you like and discard the thing you don't," says Steel. They are able to edit what inspires them with speed and precision – an invaluable skill for designers confronted by London's continual visual stimulation.

After only a year in practice a mutual friend introduced HarrimanSteel to Eley Kishimoto. From this chance encounter a mutually beneficial relationship developed that continues to grow in strength. Known as the 'patron saints of print', Eley Kishimoto are primarily a womenswear label but have been particularly successful in translating their playful aesthetic across a wide range of accessories and homeware. Like HarrimanSteel they are creatively prolific and explore art, architecture and other areas less travelled by fashion designers. This common ground provided a creative foundation on which to build the relationship.

The development of a 'views-paper' was an innovative step towards a new form of communication for Eley Kishimoto. Produced in a traditional newspaper format, it was initially seen as being complementary to the brand: a "family album of collaborators" the lookbook editors note. An aesthetic exploration rather than a documentation of the collection, it showed a cross-section of what inspired Eley Kishimoto, and was distributed as promotional material to all the collaborators' clients. The newspaper format was always considered to be organic, and naturally evolved to function as a catwalk memento and subsequent lookbook. "These were far from traditional lookbooks. One issue didn't show any product, just patterns. Two issues used the original pencil sketches of the collection. It wasn't until issue four that we began to use real images of the clothes."

The use of newsprint, inspired by researching the Eley Kishimoto archives, gave the project a distinctive, raw aesthetic which HarrimanSteel felt would emphasize the brand's craft and traditional values. "We felt this approach would cut through in the glossy world of fashion," says Steel. HarrimanSteel continue to produce Eley Kishimoto's lookbooks but these are now in a more conventional and premium format that reflects the progression of the brand. Steel maintains it is still possible for the newspaper version to be revisited in the future.

HarrimanSteel are adamant that collaboration is vital to achieve the full potential of every project, regardless of the creative background of the client. "The cross-fertilization of ideas is what we do. It is about establishing human relationships and dialogue. We are not always right, the client is not always right; if both parties can acknowledge this then we are off to a pretty good start. The best clients will make your work better," says Steel. A great benefit of the long-term relationship with Eley Kishimoto is that a natural shorthand has developed. Collective responsibility plays into this as HarrimanSteel use initiative and past experience to anticipate possible strengths and weaknesses in their proposals. While this insight is irreplaceable, Steel maintains that the ultimate goal is to stay positive, to ensure that the design process remains enjoyable and does not become a battle.

While a close rapport has been established with Eley Kishimoto, Steel approaches each project for them with fresh eyes. "A chair, a table, a blank piece of paper and a pen. No preconceptions." This integrity and dedication characterize HarrimanSteel's highly constructive attitude. Thriving on broad creative challenges, they have been able to maintain an enthusiasm for their work and, importantly, their clients.

Autumn/Winter 2001/02 saw the first incarnation of the Eley Kishimoto 'views-paper' that ran to over 28 pages of full colour. "We created a collective newspaper where artists, designers, photographers and writers who are friends and collaborators of Eley Kishimoto could contribute." As a means of extending the global reach of the publication the cover featured flags from around the world with the currency equivalents of its symbolic cost of 21p. This concept was consistent in future issues and the Spring/Summer 2003 edition was extended to Old English emblems as a reference to the collection.

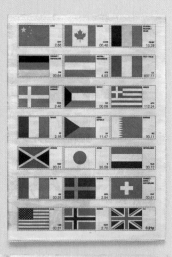

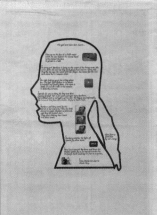

Lookbooks HARRIMANSTEEL for ELEY KISHIMOTO

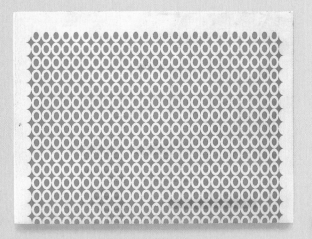

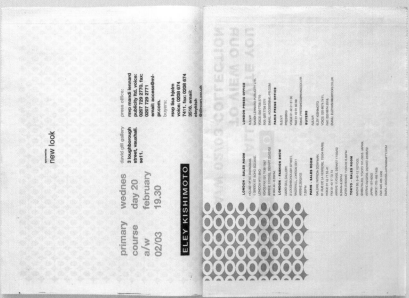

shared motivation for getting through the day
shared exhilaration with every personal discovery
shared anxiety, but hope spring's eternal
shared passion for the modern innovation
exhausted with joy

communal prescience
an exchange of ideas in the workplace
passing remarks clutched from the ether
given life by another's breath
and returned to you

a school of thought acknowledges the past
- no looking back.
at the pinnacle of the pyramid, i can see for miles…
and although today's new is tomorrow's old hat for
your kids to discard
the friends who created those moments forged true
bonds for life

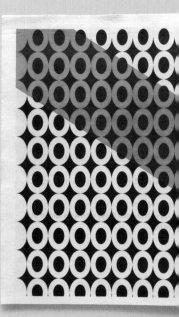

Lookbooks HARRIMANSTEEL for ELEY KISHIMOTO

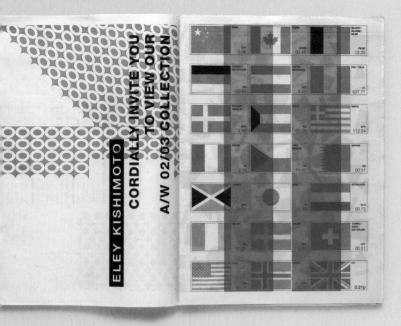

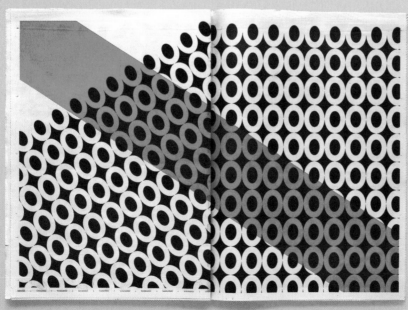

The spreads from Autumn/Winter 2002/03 emphasize the importance of conveying the inspirations of Eley Kishimoto in addition to the garments from the collection. "The idea came from researching the archives of the label and discovering their passion for print, drawing and silkscreen."

Lookbooks HARRIMANSTEEL for ELEY KISHIMOTO

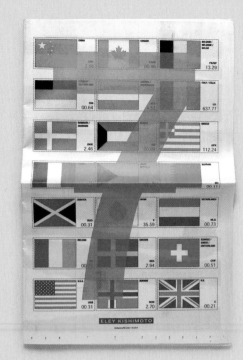

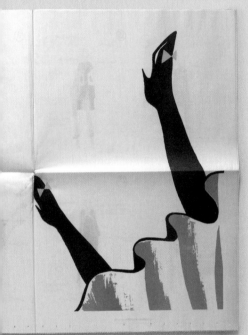

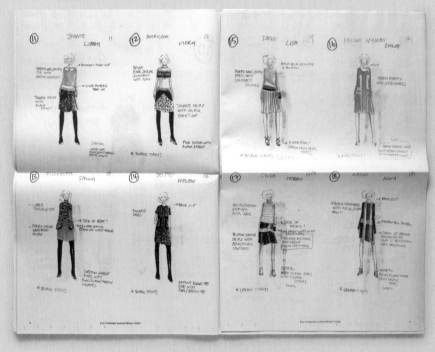

"These were far from traditional lookbooks. One issue didn't show any product, just patterns. Two issues used the original pencil sketches of the collection. It wasn't until issue four that we began to use real images of the clothes." Autumn/Winter 2003/04 is an example of the shift to broadsheet format that indicated the second stage of the concept and fulfilled the role of the lookbook by offering images or illustrations of the collection. The illustrations are strikingly similar to the looks of the final collection.

Lookbooks **HARRIMANSTEEL** for **ELEY KISHIMOTO**

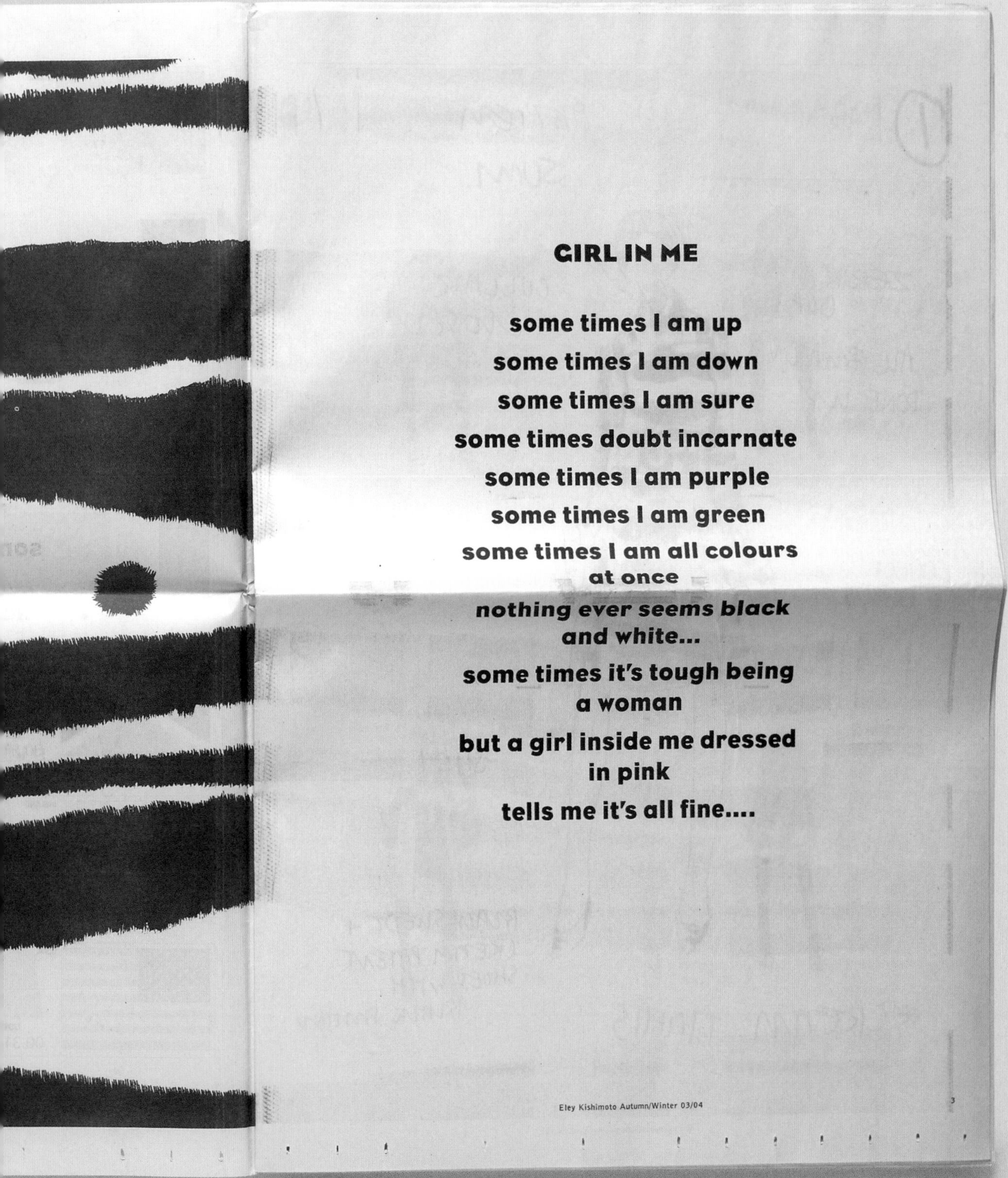

GIRL IN ME

some times I am up

some times I am down

some times I am sure

some times doubt incarnate

some times I am purple

some times I am green

some times I am all colours
at once

nothing ever seems *black*
and white...

some times it's tough being
a woman

but a girl inside me dressed
in pink

tells me it's all fine....

Eley Kishimoto Autumn/Winter 03/04

3

JOHAN HJERPE for DIANA ORVING

Johan Hjerpe explores "images, objects and spatiality" with passion as he strives to translate the underlying narratives of his clients into designs. "In general I see design as props or a set design that position and support clients and consumers in their narratives. In other words I don't like design that tries to 'communicate' in an ad sense. 'Communication' demands memorizing, props are useful tools." This is the core of his creative intentions – to maintain the practicality and relevance of his output.

Hjerpe started his studio in Stockholm in 2004, and considers fashion to be a "small but ambitious" component of the city's creative industry. At college he collaborated with the fashion and product design departments, which stimulated his interest in these fields and encouraged a broader creative awareness. The experience undoubtedly informed his sensitivity to the fashion industry's requirements and its demand for "understanding and respect for its uniqueness".

Hjerpe finds personal satisfaction in the everyday details of processing a design, but is careful to remain focused on the end result. He is careful not to form initial conclusions or become over-confident about the direction a project should take. He is an intuitive practitioner, confident that his work is successful "when there is nothing to say about it, no easy point of improvement. Everything is very clear but why or how is very hard to put in words. You can feel sort of an intense complexity but it's hard to identify the building blocks."

Diana Orving's creativity goes beyond the production of garments. Every season, in fashion shows that are more akin to theatre, she invites her audience to take an emotional journey. She develops detailed narratives that unfold with every piece of her collection, emphasizing the importance of the complete integration of the graphic design into her practice. Orving and Hjerpe have worked together since 2003, and have developed an impenetrable collaborative partnership. "It is hard to say where the collection ends and the graphic design begins for me. My work for Diana is always an extension of the collection," says Hjerpe.

There appears to be a seamless exchange of ideas between them, supported by mutual respect. Constant dialogue is vital as Hjerpe is active early in the creative process in order to produce a definitive response to the narrative of a collection. Conventional professional roles are abandoned in exchange for collective contribution. "Diana has a great sensibility for the subtlety of a typeface and how it is treated. This makes it a sometimes demanding but potentially great collaboration. You can't hide behind your experience – you have to use it." By the same token, Hjerpe has ventured into fashion: he developed prints for the Autumn/Winter 2007/08 collection that were translated into the central graphic element for the lookbook.

Visual literacy is the foundation of their relationship, and allows the dialogue to flow easily over references, materials and potential visual cues. "The visual testing ground cannot be translated into words without losing precision, at least not before the start. Later in the process it is good to verbalize in order to evaluate the direction," says Hjerpe. For Spring/Summer 2006 Orving explored seven standard garments in different sizes, playing with the concept of scale. While they were technically simplistic, the lookbook extended the collection beautifully, with standard page formats and black-and-white laser printing. Although it was conceptually justified, Hjerpe feels this is not enough to consider the project a complete success. "I feel that concepts need to be 'unsmarted' and taken to poetic heights as well."

More than dedicated to self-improvement, Hjerpe is forward thinking and has a natural creative curiosity that drives his work. "For me work and leisure are very hard to separate." Uninhibited by conventional modes of creativity, when Hjerpe is secure in a constructive and stimulating working relationship, such as with Diana Orving, he is able to draw the best from himself and his client. While there are no prerequisites for someone so adaptive, collaboration in this instance has certainly been essential to the results.

www.johanhjerpe.com
www.dianaorving.com

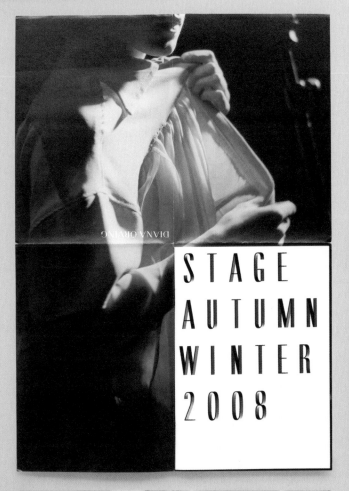

During a period of six months I worked regularly with four actors. We spoke about our clothes. About our dreams and shortcomings. About our secrets. Memories. Strategies. How to dress oneself as someone else. On stage. And how we dress ourselves as ourselves everyday. What we choose to wear and not wear. The autumn winter collection has grown out of these meetings.

The collection shows the actors in an appearance that was also the result of our meetings. The stage was Elverket, the experimental stage of the Royal dramatic theatre in Stockholm. The pictures you see here were taken during the meetings by the photographer Martina Hoogland Ivanov.

Heartfelt thanks to the actors Charlotte Engelkes, Rebecka Hemse, Hulda Lind Jóhannsdóttir och Livia Millhagen.

/ Diana Orving

The cover of the postcard-sized Autumn/ Winter 2008/09 lookbook folds out to reveal images by Martina Hoogland Ivanov that inspired the collection. An additional booklet with studio images of the collection is photographed by Anne Grandin.
"If life is a feature film, fashion provides the costume and graphic design the props for you to build your character and story."

Lookbooks JOHAN HJERPE for DIANA ORVING

SCARF

DIANA ORVING

Showroom at NEU, Nytorgsgatan 36, Stockholm.
Please call for appointment.

+46 739 38 89 79

info@dianaorving.com

Photography: Daniel Skoog

Styling: Naomi Itkes

Hair: Erika Svedjevik

Make-up: Sara Denman

Set design: Tova Rudin-Lundell, Johan Hjerpe

Model: Charlotte Hurtig

Production Assistant: Pernilla Rozenberg

Art Direction and Design: Johan Hjerpe

0-S-S-06   —

*"For Spring/Summer 2006 Diana made
a collection based on seven standard
garments (shirt, trousers, vest, etc.) in
the standard sizes of S-M-L. The small
shirt, for example, became more of a
bolero; while the large shirt was so large
it became a dress. My printing budget
basically left me with copier paper and
a laser printer. We named the collection
'STANDARD-S-S-06' and I kept everything
as standard as I could with stock A5–A3
papers and black laser printing. The cheap
production kept the collection high-end
because of the conceptual fit."*

L—   —

DIANA ORVING

www.dianaorving.com

The Autumn/Winter 2007/08 lookbook features photography by Erik Wåhlström and an illustration by Johan Hjerpe on the reverse that was also used as a fabric print in the collection. "I have an ongoing feeling that the ultimate work philosophy is just around the corner. Each new project seems to demand a portion of redefining though – and next corner it is."

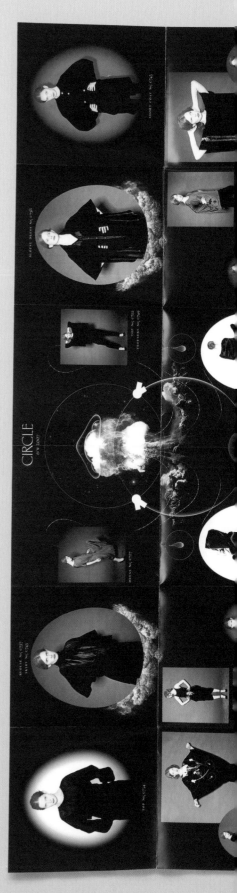

CIRCLE
a/w 2007

JULIA BORN for JOFF

The ability to translate content into a visual form is a dominant feature in the work of Swiss designer Julia Born. She founded her practice in Amsterdam immediately after graduation in 2000, and approaches each project without preconceived formal restrictions. She allows the content and context of each project to provide the framework from which to work. Born works alone yet often collaborates with other graphic designers to offer greater flexibility and broaden her creativity. Her working method starts with careful analysis of the material and systematic deconstruction of existing rules before she assembles the content into a fully integrated message. JOFF shares in this process of "deconstruction and reconstruction."

JOFF is the fashion label and alter ego of Born's long-term friend and collaborator Joffrey Moolhuizen. Having first met in college, they have since developed a creative partnership which is the complete opposite of the conventional designer/client structure. "The collaborative aspect is the core of the relationship. I never regarded him as a client, he was always a partner; he also never regarded me as a graphic designer whom he has commissioned. We are very much part of each other's process," says Born. There is no structured brief, ideas flow from their conversations and are completely free of any commercial pressures.

While working as individual practitioners, their friendship facilitates spontaneous creative innovation. "We have a similar understanding of concepts and ideas. On one hand we speak the same language, on the other we are quite different. I try to analyze and build systems where Joff works with a conceptual idea and makes a lot of intuitive decisions in his process." While developing their own independent visual aesthetic, they share a conceptual process that allows greater awareness and integration in their collaboration.

JOFF exists outside the commercial demands of the fashion industry as an irregular participant, pursuing a singular vision rather than subscribing to the cyclical nature of fashion. More in step with the art establishment, JOFF is an attempt to redefine the rules of fashion, discovering an alternative format within the strict hierarchy. For Autumn/ Winter 2005/06, JOFF presented the Ofoffjoff collection as part of Dutch Touch New York. Conceived as an exercise in reducing the fashion industry from the scale of the global to individual, ten outfits were presented in one size, Moolhuizen's size, his 'measure for all'. The collection challenged the fleeting nature of fashion trends by selling the garments immediately from the catwalk. Because the collection did not go into production, the limited quantities created immediate appeal. This subversion of fashion commercialism brought a truly personal touch and an honest self-awareness rarely seen in the industry.

Rather than a simple documentation of the collection, 'Ofoffjoff – One to One' is an independent project, an extension in print format that creates new compositions and important juxtapositions. The book explores the human body as a landscape, and more accurately the landscape of fashion. Life-size reproductions of Moolhuizen's collection appear in a book format. "It is not a conventional catalogue, it is a piece in itself," says Born. The exercise was extended into a photographic exhibition and then reinterpreted back into book format. "What is important about this project and crucial to the collaboration is that it is never ending, it transforms itself over and over. The translation into different media is very important and something we find very interesting." Going far beyond the restrictions of a conventional fashion collection or lookbook, the project continues to progress and the concept has become a source of continual innovation.

Born does not actively seek such close collaborations but they seem to occur naturally as a result of her passion for the exchange of ideas and creative overlap. The intimacy of her relationship with JOFF is not easily replicated yet the requirement of constructive, open communication is vital. "In all my work it is crucial to establish a constructive dialogue with my client. If it is not possible, then I cannot work with them." Born approaches every project with equal enthusiasm, aiming to uncover the unique requirements of each client and satisfy them with measured, creative innovation.

www.juliaborn.com
www.joff.nl

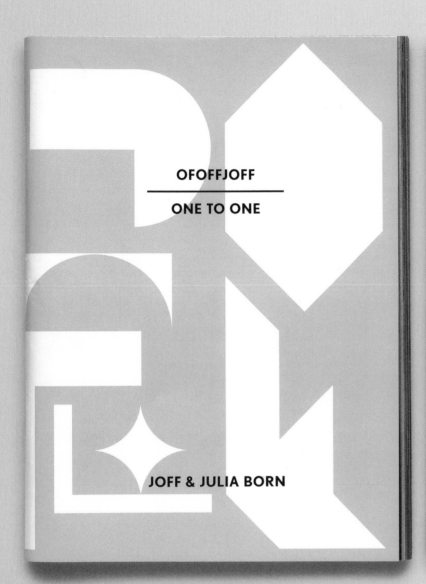

OFOFFJOFF
—————————
ONE TO ONE

JOFF & JULIA BORN

'OFOFFJOFF – ONE TO ONE' IS A SEQUEL PROJECT TO 'OFOFFJOFF', THE ONE-OFF COLLECTION BY DUTCH FASHION DESIGNER JOFF, WHIC[H] WAS PRESENTED – OR BETTER YET PERFORMED – DURING THE FALL 2005 FASHION WEEK IN NEW YORK AND LATER THAT YEAR WITH A SIMILAR PERFORMANCE AND INSTANT JOFF-SHOP IN AMSTERDAM.

WITH THIS PUBLICATION, JOFF AND LONG TIME COLLABORATOR GRAPHIC DESIGNER JULIA BORN, REPEAT THEIR BRAVE WHISPER OF A FASHION STATEMENT; PRESENTING JOFF'S OWN IMAGE LIFE-SIZ[E] JUST LIKE THE 'OFOFFJOFF' COLLECTION WHICH WAS CONCEIVED IN HIS IMAGE AS WELL AS IN HIS SIZE ONLY.

THIS ONE-OFF COLLECTION, WHICH WAS SOLD TO FRIENDS, FANS AND COLLECTORS RIGHT AFTER THE PERFORMANCE, WAS EXTREMELY EXCLUSIVE, A PEER-TO-PEER AFFAIR. KNOWING AND LOVING JOFF, EXPRESSING HIMSELF IN HIS WORK, BECOMES REFLECTING HIS IMAG[E] AND CONTRIBUTING TO HIS MICRO CREATIVE ECONOMY. IT IS THE EXTREME REDUCTION OF SCALE, FROM A GLOBAL SCALE TO A ONE-TO[-] ONE SCALE, THAT MAKES THE STATEMENT BRAVE AND VALUABLE IN OUR TIME. AS FASHION TODAY IS ABOUT 'IMAGE' AND 'EXCLUSIVITY' ONLY, JOFF AND JULIA BORN PRESENT US WITH AN ULTIMATE.

'OFOFFJOFF – ONE TO ONE' IS MORE THAN AN ENCORE ON PAPE[R] THE CLASSIC MEDIUM TO LET FASHION TRANSCEND BEYOND THE ORIGINAL OBJECT OF DESIRE, LIKE FOR INSTANCE A CATALOGUE OR LOOK BOOK AS IT IS CALLED IN FASHION. 'OFOFFJOFF – ONE TO ONE' IS A FASHION OBJECT IN ITSELF, GIVING THE AUDIENCE AN ALTERNATIVE TO DISCOVER IN DETAIL AS WELL AS RELATE TO JOFF'S DESIGNS, HIS STYLE, HIS IMAGE, HIS SIZE, ONE-TO-ONE. JOFF AND YO[U] MUCH LIKE EARLY POP MAGAZINES FEATURED LIFE-SIZE 'STARSCHNIT[T]' IMAGES OF TEENAGE ICONS, IN THIS PUBLICATION THE DESIGNER AGAIN BECOMES THE MEASURE OF ALL.

CONCEPT AND DESIGN	TEXT	DISTRIBUTION
JULIA BORN & JOFF	MO VELD	WWW.IDEABOOKS.[NL]
COLLECTION	PRINTING	CONTACT
OFOFFJOFF BY JOFF	DRUKKERIJ CALFF & MEISCHKE	WWW.JOFF.NL
MODEL	EDITION	ISBN
JOFF	750 COPIES	978-90-9021583-9
PHOTOGRAPHY	WITH THE KIND SUPPORT OF	COPYRIGHT
ANUSCHKA BLOMMERS & NIELS SCHUMM	THE NETHERLANDS FOUNDATION FOR VISUAL ARTS, DESIGN & ARCHITECTURE; IDEAL BERLIN; DRUKKERIJ CALFF & MEISCHKE	© 2007 THE AUTHO[RS] THE PHOTOGRAPHE[R] REPRODUCTION W[ITHOUT] PERMISSION PROH[IBITED]

"The concept for the design is very simple: we show ten life-sized photographs throughout the book. The cut-up posters, piled up and folded together into the book generate a dramaturgy and layout where new combinations and figures are invented on each spread. It's almost a remake – a 'Part 2' as it were – of the collection itself with new pieces of clothing, poses, fabrics, etc. The system of compiling is subtly visible when the 'narrative' goes from head, down to feet, and back again."

Ten life-sized, black-and-white images by Anuschka Blommers and Niels Schumm are spread over 192 pages of the 23 x 31-cm (9 x 12¼-in) lookbook. Mo Veld provides supporting text on the back cover.

MANUEL RAEDER for BLESS

While Berlin-based Manuel Raeder provides the traditional services of a graphic design studio, his work transcends the printed page to enter the public consciousness. The defining focus of his practice is on content and concept, with the result that form is relegated to the periphery of his creative process. Stripped of visual distraction, Raeder's aesthetic has an honesty that forces the audience to look beyond the surface and interact directly with the content.

In-depth and constant dialogue is vital to achieving this creative distillation, both within his studio environment and with his clients. "Everything I work on and do, I consider a collaboration," says Raeder. This emphasis on collaboration and on taking the process beyond the object is also at the core of what motivates BLESS. Neither designer nor client is limited by a single traditional discipline: the breadth of their interest and talent means they continually look for new opportunities and forms of expression.

Challenging the perceptions of their audience is central to the aesthetic of BLESS. The ability to see every decision as a unique opportunity for creative intervention, free from established conventions, is the driving force behind their process. There is a beauty and simplicity to their lookbooks, which are published within a different 'host' fashion magazine each season. Rather than approach them as a simple design problem, BLESS have carved out an alternative to conventional fashion advertising and lookbook distribution. Beyond the economy of combining these two key aspects of communication, this creates heightened expectation, a broader audience and inherent collectability. Raeder says that more than producing just a lookbook, they are trying to "join together new friends or make unusual encounters happen".

The lookbooks are supplementary to, or completely integrated into, the 'host' magazine. They change physical location, distribution and format every season. Throughout this fluctuation, Raeder has maintained a sense of continuity by adopting a rigid set of photographic principles. Although professional photographers are employed, their images are put through a 'collective' editing process. From participants on the catwalk to friends in the audience, a broad range of photographic material is collected and then edited down. Disregarding the beauty of the images, Raeder and BLESS deconstruct them to their base components to analyze whether they are viable for publication in the lookbook. This rigorous process yields cohesive results season after season.

Raeder's ability to achieve such a close and productive collaboration with his client is ultimately a key factor in the success of the lookbooks. Rather than breaking down conventions there is a complete lack of acceptance of predetermined solutions; and even within the cyclical nature of fashion, Raeder and BLESS see this process with an objective clarity, recognising that every situation is new and requires a unique solution.

www.manuelraeder.co.uk
www.bless-service.de

The 11th issue of Pacemaker from March 2006 hosted the combined N°28 'Climate Confusion Assistance' and N°29 'Wallscapes' BLESS lookbook. The A2 poster format was folded down to A5 in the same way as the host magazine. "The presentation of the new collection happened in Paris during fashion week inside a gallery in front of wallpapers by BLESS. Due to that we designed two posters printed back and front, with images mixed of the wallscapes and the presentation. Almost like opening up another space, making the confusion between where the model's are standing and where the wallpapers with BLESS objects start even more confusing." Photography was included by Carl Henrik Tillberg Maria Ziegeiböck, Cécile Bortoletti, Jelena Rundqvist, Nadège Baudon, Irene Leung, Sonny, Heinz Peter Knes and BLESS.

PARIS LA

Issue #1
Winter 2008/2009
8 Euro

Do.Pé.

A
FASHION
BLOGZINE
BASED IN
THE DARKNESS
OF THE
ENCHANTED
FOREST
SURROUNDED
BY ELECTROBIRDSONGS

2008
review

In a book published on the occasion of his show at Galerie Vallois,
series of snapshots taken just as his innocent victims take their fir
bite of the repulsive canned burger conveys the existential horror
bad food inspires in the French. Mortified, in a paralysis of fear, th
unsuspecting shoppers have no choice but to swallow the meat, at
somehow it's in this weird and slightly violent exchange that
Bouchet's peculiar genius is apparent. We know that ultimately th

mixing. Despoliate money from an emotion except anger. Take it.
Take the consequences, like a (na hard way, Take it, take a like a
man. Give it to the Pain. Poverty grants clarity, Poverty reinforces a
strictly conceal medico radiating space/hous, events, predu. A...
awareness and welcoming of death. Approach death. Live with death.

"If music be the food of love, play on"
quote from Shakespeare play "Twelfth Night, or What You Will." Act I, Sc.1

FIELD OF LOVE

FRIDAY, DECEMBER 21, 2007 — review

Scout Niblett's 4th album is out now and she
performs at Nouveau Casino, Paris this week.
Just the perfect time to say few words about her
touching sounds.

As a matter of fact, singer **Scout Niblett** knows how to feed her
people. A pure punk-folk icon, she could be the natural sister of Kurt
Cobain, R.I.P. She's scratching the bass like a rock star, clapping the
drums like a foolish girl, and whispering words with a deep dear dark
crystal voice. Shifting between a gentle ghost and a broken-winged
angel during her live performances, she plays music with truth and
honesty.

For our own salvation, Emma aka Scout Niblett, is back with a
magnificent new album (her 4th), featuring another great poet, Sir
Will Oldham aka Bonnie "Prince" Billie. "This Fool Can New Die," an
album that could be easily compare to a modern Shakespeare play
both in words and meaning, brings warm affection into a world where
it's sometimes missing. Always questioning about fragile feelings into
somehow succeeds like a magic writer to stand up and fight with love
against emotion and dedication. Songs like "Dinosaur Egg" or
"Hide and Seek" recall old epic poems and reinforce at the same time
a demonstration of non-obeissance. And even if the songs often start
as her music can go crazy in breaking the waves. With "Moon Lake"
and "Let Think Heart Be Warmest", maybe the tracks that sound the
most like her beautifully rough earlier albums, drums & guitar give
enough strength to inspire rebellion in any kind of savel.

Although Scout Niblett always clearly wants to "Comfort You" like a
kind-hearted queen, she gives emotion and tears that amazingly
bring good feelings with ease. This is her way to become the prince
she pretended to be in her song "I'll be Your Prince" on the "I am"
album. With a humble attitude and a pure iconic style, Scout Niblett
reaches the sky again and brings back a piece of stone. She's simply
one of the greatest! <p>

further information see Scout Niblett

T
°36 Nothingneath.
2009 catalog

R
posts from Do.Pé.,
blogzine based in the
of the enchanted forest

YS
AMI QUI VOUS
U BIEN. p2
Marcopolous
rice Paineau they
anything but
re

S YOU ARE. p88
eld reviews
olette

ON
ANS PARIS. p12
ux
UN AIR LÉGER. p20
Rivrain
E TO
EAN. p30
atki
POINT. p64
Sandberg

NG
UR COOPER. p44
per, a coffee without
with Oscar Tuazon

HE VIP ROOM. p56
LA with
ødland

D
HORIZONS. p72
by Camille Vivier
le

GOES
S. p40
nk rock band are
inner in Paris /
y Amy Yao
LABOR. p90
kers, a French
oad / Photograph
Schwoerer

BLESS N° 36 Nothingneath

180

Lookbooks MANUEL RAEDER for BLESS

The N°36 'Nothingneath' collection lookbook was a loose insert into the centrefold of the first issue of Paris LA in Winter 2008/09. Slightly smaller than the host magazine, the 20 x 27-cm (7¾ x 10½-in) lookbook featured images of the models by Heinz Peter Knes gathered on the narrow staircase of Hôtel Particulier in Paris.

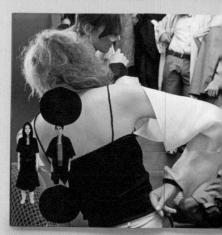

The N°27 'Eased Up' presentation took place in a Paris flower market. Running over the final 33 pages of the Spring/Summer 2006 issue of Textfield IV, the lookbook formed the only colour pages in the whole magazine. Referencing the growth and decline of flowers, the images fluctuate in size before presenting every look from the collection as a grid on the inside back cover. Photography was included by Cécile Bortoletti, Christian Badger, Manuel Raeder and BLESS.

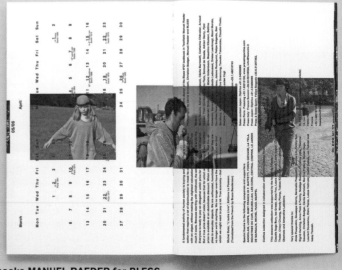

Lookbooks MANUEL RAEDER for BLESS

As the most explicit example of integrating with the host magazine, elements of the N°32 'Frustverderber' collection lookbook feature on every page of the sixth issue of Monthly Vampire from 2007. Restricted predominately to the lower central quadrant of the page, the lookbook slowly builds up to a temporary full spread where it becomes completely incorporated into the editorial content. Photography was included by Heinz Peter Knes, Bernd Kaag, Samuel de Goede, Cécile Bortoletti, Jean Yves Giot and BLESS.

Lookbooks MANUEL RAEDER for BLESS

Display_Seoul Museum of Art, 2004
c-print, 180x220cm

c. Kim Sanggil

Display_Leeum, Samsung Museum of Art #03, 2007
c-print, 180x220cm

c. Kim Sanggil

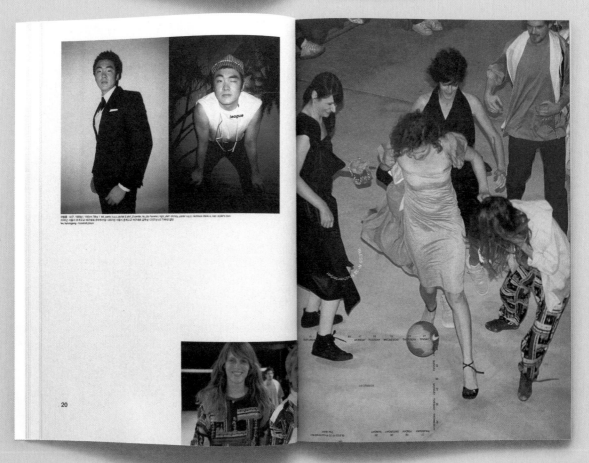

78

As an extension of the lookbook, Raeder incorporates The Dater to "provide a sense of space and time, future and past". The Dater (shown here at the bottom of the left-hand page) is fully integrated into each lookbook, providing the reader with relevant, sometimes personal dates of importance for BLESS in the coming months. Sometimes empty, the format also encourages the readers to add their own information.

Each season Raeder is commissioned to collaborate with BLESS on a fabric pattern. Derived from the graphic design of the previous season lookbook, the fabric is then integrated by BLESS into the 'Last Season T-shirt' for the current collection. Acting as both conceptual reference point and integration between the cyclical seasons of fashion, this side project possibly best illustrates the strength of their collaboration and the break with the conventional designer/client relationship.

79

PLUG-IN GRAPHIC for
ARTS&SCIENCE

Plug-In Graphic have refined the ability to translate visual language into a complete tactile experience. Their combination of sensitive typography and accessible imagery with specialized materials and production techniques results in end products that are immediately familiar and comfortable. This is achieved through painstaking attention to detail at every stage of the design process to ensure the desired effect is realized. The Tokyo-based studio's dedication and commitment is due to the enthusiasm of founder Naomi Hirabayashi, who infuses every project with a personal touch.

Similarly, the Japanese label Arts&Science is an extension of the personal vision of its founder, Sonya S. Park. Focused on exquisite materials and fine craftsmanship, the luxury brand captures the comfort of a simple way of life within a contemporary framework. Seasonal but not trend-based, Arts&Science offer an aspirational lifestyle of basic garments, accessories and homeware products (even biscuits). In contrast to the perceived exclusivity of fashion labels, they embrace collaboration, and other premium labels are sold in their retail stores to reinforce the depth and authenticity of their brand values.

Hirabayashi has been retained by Arts&Science since the studio's launch in 2003. During this successful relationship she has produced all the label's print collateral and developed a range of unique yet collectively balanced logos to identify the diffusion lines. In a reversal of conventional practice, Hirabayashi initiates proposals to Arts&Science for projects she thinks are required. Her ideas are evaluated solely on the basis of their suitability to the brand, with no budgetary considerations. "I think you could call this a collaboration rather than the usual relationship between a client and a graphic designer," says Hirabayashi. More than trust or respect, the success of this collaboration relies on shared creative ownership.

Constructive dialogue is vital to achieving this and is in part made possible through a common visual language. However, according to Hirabayashi, a creative background is not a prerequisite for a successful relationship and can at times become an obstacle. She believes it is more important for clients to have a clear vision of what they want to achieve and the ability to remain objective throughout the design process. This can be difficult for creative clients who tend to have more emotional investment in a project than more commercially based companies. For Hirabayashi, Arts&Science represent the perfect balance: "The owner is creative and also a talented marketer. Rather than spending a large percentage of the budget on advertising she knows it is more meaningful to spend time and money on catalogues and other marketing tools. In that respect we have the best kind of relationship possible between a graphic designer and client."

While Hirabayashi draws inspiration from the past, she is fascinated by Swiss typography, which provides the perfect technical counterbalance to the warmth of her projects. "I often find hints for typestyles and textures on old printed matter or packages." Hirabayashi insists there is no formula to her creative process as every client presents unique challenges. Her focus with Arts&Science is to build a message that is "high-quality, classic yet modern, genderless", to reflect the label's understated luxury and accessible refinement. The imagery in the lookbooks is warm and textured, and there is an expectation that the visual will have the strength to convey more than simply the look and style of a garment. The lookbooks are visually warm and textured. The photography has the strength to convey more than simply the look and style of a garment. Illustrated references and supporting text are isolated on the pages that follow the photographic spreads. Embossing, foil blocking and speciality paper are often used to enrich the tactility of the lookbooks.

The clear harmony between Arts&Science's products and their visual communication appears to be logical and effortless. A true indicator of success, this natural simplicity conceals the complexity and sophistication of the message. With seemingly parallel aesthetics, the real strength of the relationship between designer and client lies in the commitment and trust of both parties. Hirabayashi's passion and raw talent are why clients seek her out and, undoubtedly, why she becomes invaluable to them.

Delivered in a custom-designed envelope, there is an effortless beauty to the images from the Spring/Summer 2009 lookbook that appear frozen in time. Satoshi Yamaguchi has a long-standing relationship with Plug-In Graphic and photographs all the work for Arts&Science. "Paper of such thinness has been used so that it looks as if the printing can also be seen from the back. The catalogue was made without a cover so that it looks like a book still in the process of being made. It is of a very simple structure, with the photos of the products and the credits being placed on different pages and inserted alternately."

www.plug-in.co.uk
www.arts-science.com

NUMBER:
001

BRAND:
A&S
ITEM:
Maxi Coat
PRICE:
¥92,400
MATERIAL:
55% Wool, 45% Cotton
SIZE:
1, 2
COLOR:
Black

The Autumn/Winter 2005/06 lookbook
skilfully balances textures, multiple paper
stocks and variable page sizes. "Smooth,
elegant, cream-coloured paper has been
used, and the cover decorated with a pale
green band. On the band is the embossed
shape of a large emblem, which is the
motif for this brand."

ARTS & SCIENCE
— EST. IN 21ST CENTURY —

2007–2008
AUTUMN and WINTER COLLECTION

http://www.arts-science.com

VOLUME EIGHT.

AOYAMA
Pacific Aoyama,
6.6.20 Minami Aoyama Minato-ku
Tokyo 107.0062 Japan
Telephone: 81 3 3498 1091
arts-2@arts-science.com

DAIKANYAMA
100 Daikanyama-ivy
9.3 Daikanyamacho Shibuya-ku
Tokyo 150.0034 Japan
Telephone: 81 3 5459 6375
arts@arts-science.com

MARUNOUCHI
1F, Shin-Marunouchi Building
1.5.1 Marunouchi Chiyoda-ku
Tokyo 100.6501 Japan
Telephone: 81 3 5224 8651
arts-m@arts-science.com

SHOES and THINGS
103 Palace Aoyama,
6.1.6 Minami Aoyama Minato-ku
Tokyo 107.0062 Japan
Telephone: 81 3 3499 7601
arts-shoes@arts-science.com

DISPLAY
Palace Miyuki,
5.3.8 Minami Aoyama Minato-ku
Tokyo 107.0062 Japan
Telephone: 81 3 3400 1009
display@arts-science.com

There is an open warmth to the editorial voice used on the cover of the Autumn Winter 2007/08 lookbook. "All the photos have been printed by offset printing, and the gold letters have then been printed by letterpress. The combination of offset printing with letterpress can create a distinctive look. It is a method we like and often use. To make it easier for the reader to choose products, the products have been sorted into four categories, and the pages designed to look indexed." The envelope reveals the visual balance between the logos of all the diffusion lines.

PLUG-IN GRAPHIC for
JOURNAL STANDARD

In 2001, after receiving widespread acclaim for her work in the creative department of a leading cosmetics brand, Naomi Hirabayashi wanted to explore a broader range of creative challenges and decided to start her own studio. She believes breadth of knowledge is vital to graphic design, and has been able to translate this belief into a wide range of clients for Plug-In Graphic, her Tokyo-based studio. The name signifies the "connecting of something to something", emphasizing the role of graphic design as a mediator between clients and consumers.

Journal Standard is a contemporary Japanese fashion brand with a range of diffusion lines. Referencing classical, well-heeled Western quality, Luxe is a premium womenswear range that disregards trends to focus on a complete lifestyle experience. Retail outlets stock the Journal Standard Luxe collection and a select range of other luxury brands; interiors are luxurious yet based on modest home comforts. Eclectic vintage furniture gives warmth and authenticity to sumptuous fabrics and fine craftsmanship. Hirabayashi has directly translated this aesthetic into the company's lookbooks, extending the consumer experience in a very personal way.

Initially inspired by old photographs, Hirabayashi considers the key elements of the lookbooks to be "well-used, high-quality items and nostalgia". The garments are subverted by the sheer beauty of the imagery. The Spring/Summer 2009 lookbook, *The Popular Encyclopedia of 'Herbal Trap'*, is influenced by academic literature. The text on the opening pages is set on natural, uncoated paper, and, with its scientific definitions, is angled more towards botany than fashion. Glossy, central pages feature colour and black-and-white images of models wearing the garments; supplementary details and interior shots build atmosphere. The final pages return to natural stock and reference an appendix table with details of each garment. The overall effect is in stark contrast to a conventional sales vehicle: the lookbook is a direct extension of Journal Standard Luxe's brand values and visual aesthetic. To promote the exclusivity of the lookbooks the cover of each one is numbered to indicate that it is part of a limited edition.

Almost more than the garments and accessories, narrative is central to the company's brand communication and is crucial to attracting and retaining customers. While the lookbooks offer all the staple requirements of their conventional counterparts, they are buried under a thick layer of style that turns the hard sell into a personal invitation.

Attention to detail is standard for Hirabayashi and is essential to creating the subtle authenticity seen in the lookbooks. She labours over the choice of materials and production techniques to ensure the end result matches her vision. "The various problems that occur during the design process are only the concern of the designer, not other people. The final product is the only thing important for someone actually holding an item designed by me in their hands." While the message conveyed in the books is conceptually layered, Hirabayashi ensures it is clear and accessible. The precision of her execution would be obvious were it not for the refined detail and sheer desirability of the Journal Standard Luxe lookbooks – an exceptional exercise in balance.

Hirabayashi believes the idea that fashion offers more creative freedom than other markets is somewhat of a misconception: "There are more troubles with clients who have a creative background. I face disagreements often. However, the issues can be solved in most cases by talking. There is no case of one side being stronger than the other." While her relationship with Journal Standard Luxe stretches back to 2004, it is simplistic to believe that their mutual respect has only been built over time. Hirabayashi's unique aesthetic actively draws clients to her practice and they commit to her process; it is clear that her value to them is more than simply her skills in composition and material selection.

www.plug-in.co.uk
www.journal-standard.jp

There is an intimacy to the Autumn/Winter 2005/06 Journal Standard Luxe lookbook: loose sheets of apparently aged paper, in addition to variations in the trim-size, create the impression of a personal collection of curios from a time gone past. "In making this, the image we had in mind was the classic, black cartons made from there different kinds of paper. For this season's photos, we took shots of numerous stuffed animals, which we moved into a warehouse no longer in use." There is a nostalgia to the photography by Yasutomo Ebisu, who has developed a long-term collaboration with Naomi Hirabayashi. "I have been working with the same staff of cameramen, hairdressers and make-up artists for the last five years."

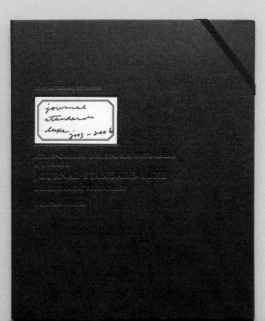

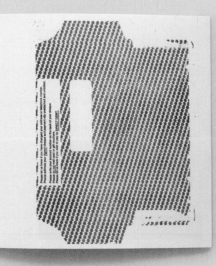

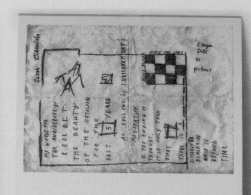

"The photos in the main text have been printed offset, while the photo and the writing on the cover have all been printed by letterpress. The catalogue was made for the fifth anniversary celebration of Journal Standard Luxe and we received congratulatory messages from various artists. We printed these messages on cotton paper by letterpress and inserted them into the catalogue, purposely letting them peep out from the pages."

Lookbooks PLUG-IN GRAPHIC for JOURNAL STANDARD

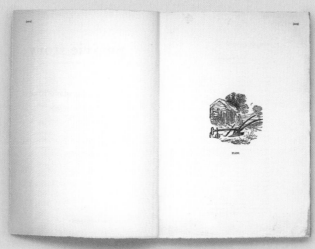

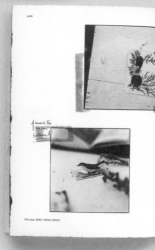

"To resemble an old French book, the edges of the pages of the Journal Standard Luxe Spring/Summer 2008 'Prairie Story' lookbook have been printed so that they appear sunburnt, and the pages have not been trimmed evenly. A printing machine was not suitable for the look we wanted, so the edges were finished by hand. After the printing and bookbinding of the catalogue had been done, the edges of the paper were burnt with a burner, and then the scorched parts were scraped off with sandpaper. The photos have been printed by offset printing, while all of the writing is printed by letterpress."

The theme for the Journal Standard Luxe 2006 collection was 'Spritual White' and so we made a pure white catalogue. The threads, case, covers and stickers on the covers used for the bookbinding were all white, but the textures were different. Even though everything was white, we were able to achieve a lovely finish because of the many varied textures. The book has been made so that it looks as if it has been turned inside out at the middle. I think that adding a slightly destructive element to an object helps to make its beauty stand out even more."

PAGE :
TWENTY SEVEN.

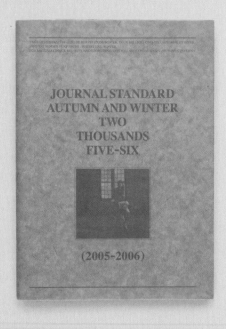

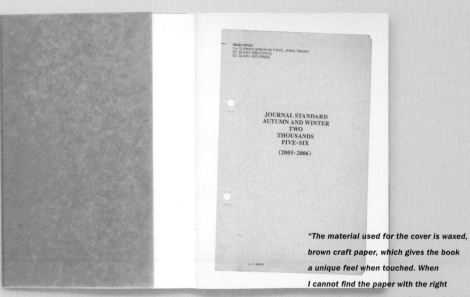

"The material used for the cover is waxed, brown craft paper, which gives the book a unique feel when touched. When I cannot find the paper with the right texture, I sometimes use printing techniques to create the ideal texture, and this is one such example." The Autumn/Winter 2005/06 Journal Standard lookbook was also embellished with scribbles on the page to establish a used aesthetic. A shift in the team saw Ryotaro Horiuchi take over the photography of the publication.

PART ONE.

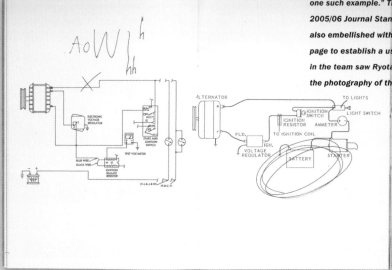

198

Lookbooks **PLUG-IN GRAPHIC for JOURNAL STANDARD**

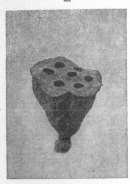

A fluctuating mix of paper stocks and contextual content builds a strong narrative around the Spring/Summer 2009 Journal Standard Luxe collection. At 17.5 x 24cm (7 x 9½in) the quarter-bound hardcover lookbook feels more academic than fashion. "A catalogue made with a botanical encyclopedia in mind. The pages at the beginning and at the end of the book are made from different paper. We placed many plants in the room and created the atmosphere of a botanical garden."

Lookbooks PLUG-IN GRAPHIC for JOURNAL STANDARD

ROSEBUD INC for UTE PLOIER

The name Rosebud Inc pays homage to the classic film *Citizen Kane* (1941). Founding partner Ralf Herms interprets this as "a mission to use each medium to its limits and explore any latent potential". Experimentation and exploration lie at the heart of the studio, which looks for original material-based solutions. Founded in Vienna in 2003, Rosebud see bespoke 'brand publishing' as a professional responsibility to their clients and outline this commitment in their manifesto. Their principled code focuses on creative innovation and prioritizes the experience of the end user at the expense of commercial motivations. While the manifesto provides the studio's orientation, it also implies that clients are expected to become active facilitators of the creative process, not merely spectators. Rosebud request participation and passion from them to ensure tailor-made results. This mutual responsibility is the basis on which all the studio's professional relationships are built.

Rosebud have produced invitations and lookbooks for Vienna-based menswear designer Ute Ploier since 2003. "The manifesto can be seen as the essence of our working ideas and ideals, a basic guideline of principles that helps us to stay focused with each and every project," says Herms. "Our relationship with Ute is an example of how our expectations of quality, uniqueness and conceptual clarity can be realized. The projects could even be considered blueprints for our manifesto."

Ploier sees each season's collection as an independent opportunity to explore the dress codes and archetypes of masculinity. Rosebud are tasked with developing a new visual language and format that suits it. Focused on function and comfort, Ploier builds her collections on a strong conceptual framework. Rosebud have the responsibility and freedom to reinterpret this and create the two-dimensional equivalent of the three-dimensional garments. From simulated holiday photographs or collage, to posters or booklets, even catwalk images, they collaborate closely with Ploier. "The conceptual approach is a *mélange* of what inspires a collection and our interpretation of the finished pieces. Ideally the main theme can be translated into a whole new format without losing the essential ingredients," says Herms.

Herms is professional, practical and compliant in his creative process. "Design is creating things based on an assignment. Problem – idea – solution." Although the relationship with Ploier is highly productive and satisfying, Herms is not convinced that creative clients necessarily initiate or extract more innovative work. While a shared creative language can be an advantage, he believes "collaboration and communication with the client is the key element for successful projects. Since fashion designers often share an equal mindset, it may be more easy to find the right vocabulary."

Confident in his process and output, Herms confesses to being "insightfully bullish" when clients need a little help in making decisions. This is only possible and successful when both parties respect each other, which he considers a prerequisite for all successful partnerships. Rosebud are supported by a manifesto that enables them to extract the best practice from their studio while drawing the client into a collaborative relationship defined by mutual responsibility.

www.rosebud-inc.com
www.uteploier.com

The Brand Publishing Manifesto

1. Brand Publishing must be done for communicating and not for selling.

2. Brand Publishing must always originate from a unique idea.

3. Only the feelings, the opinions, the beliefs of the readers are of relevance.

4. The content must never be conceived apart from the images and vice versa.

5. Naked ladies and stock images are forbidden.

6. The Publication must not contain trivial content or boring design.

7. Copying is not permitted.

8. Readers are the final and real owners of the publication.

9. Concepts must never be used more than once.

UTE PLOIER

PIONEERS

AUTUMN · WINTER 2005/06

EXPEDITION no. 160 /250

"The idea for the Autumn/Winter 2005/06 'Pioneers' lookbook was developed in close collaboration with Ute and especially the photographer Bernd Preiml. He came up with the characteristic look of the images and also did the final editing. Key to this project was the thorough focus on details, which was applied in all stages of the project: concept, photography, design and packaging. The images have been printed, laminated on cardboard, stamped and marked by hand with pens. The set of boards was packaged in a custom-made box that was finally sealed with a hand-numbered label."

UTE PLOIER

AW 07/08

THE MESSENGER

UTE PLOIER
AW 07/08
THE MESSENGER

01
SHIRT WITH TIE DETAIL:
NAVY COTTON,
TROUSERS: NAVY
COTTON, BELT: BLACK
LEATHER, FACE:
JEWELLERY SILVER

02
SHIRT: WHITE COTTON,
TROUSERS: SHINY
BLACK WOOL, 15-LOOP-
BELT: BLACK LEATHER,
GAITERS: BLACK KNIT

03
SHIRT: BLACK COTTON,
SCARF: BLACK SILK
CALF LEATHER,
TROUSERS: SHINY
BLACK WOOL, BELT:
BLACK LEATHER

04
SHIRT: WHITE COTTON,
JUMPER: BLACK KNIT,
PLEATED TROUSER:
BLACK WOOL, BELT:
BLACK LEATHER

05
SHIRT: WHITE COTTON
WITH PLEATED FRONT,
WINDBREAKER: BLACK
PLASTIC, TROUSERS:
BLACK WOOL

06
JUMPER: BLUE/BLACK
KNIT, COAT: OLIVE
COTTON, TROUSERS:
OLIVE COTTON, BAG:
BLACK LEATHER, FACE:
JEWELLERY ALUMINIUM

07
SHIRT: WHITE COTTON,
CAPE: BLACK WOOL,
TROUSERS: SHINY
BLACK WOOL, 15-LOOP-
BELT: BLACK LEATHER,
GAITERS: BLACK KNIT

08
WRAPPED SWEATER:
BLACK KNIT, TROUSERS:
BLACK WOOL

09
SHIRT: NAVY COTTON,
TROUSERS: BLACK SILK
CALF LEATHER, GLOVES:
BLACK KNIT

10
BOMBER JACKET: BLACK
SILK CALF LEATHER,
TROUSERS: SHINY
BLACK WOOL

11
SHIRT WITH TIE DETAIL:
WHITE COTTON,
CARDIGAN: DARK GREY/
BLACK KNIT, TROUSERS:
SHINY BLACK WOOL

12
SHIRT: WHITE COTTON,
COAT: BLACK LODEN,
TROUSERS: SHINY
BLACK WOOL, GAITERS:
BLACK KNIT

13
SHIRT: WHITE COTTON
WITH PLEATED FRONT,
SWEATER: BLACK
COTTON/CASHMERE
WITH SHINY PLASTIC
LINED HOOD,
TROUSERS: BLACK
WOOL

14
SHIRT: WHITE COTTON
WITH PLEATED FRONT,
SWEATER: BLACK
COTTON/CASHMERE
WITH SHINY PLASTIC
LINED HOOD,
TROUSERS: BLACK
WOOL

15
PLEATED JACKET: BLACK
WOOL, TROUSERS:
SHINY BLACK WOOL

16
SHIRT: WHITE COTTON,
CARDIGAN: GREY KNIT,
TROUSERS: NAVY
COTTON, GLOVE: GREY
KNIT

17
RAIN CAPE: SHINY
BLACK PLASTIC,
TROUSERS: BLACK
WOOL

18
SHIRT: WHITE COTTON,
JEANS WITH ZIP DETAIL:
BLACK DENIM

19
SHIRT WITH TIE DETAIL:
NAVY COTTON,
QUILTED COAT WITH
KNIT: COLLAR NAVY
COTTON, TROUSERS:
NAVY COTTON

20
SHIRT: NAVY COTTON,
PARKA: OLIVE COTTON,
TROUSERS: BLACK SILK
CALF LEATHER

21
SHIRT: NAVY COTTON,
PADDED VEST: SHINY
BLACK PLASTIC, JEANS:
BLACK DENIM, BOOT
WRAPS: BLACK PLASTIC,
FACE: JEWELLERY
SILVER

22
SHIRT: BLACK COTTON,
SUIT: BLACK SHINY
WOOL

23
SHIRT: WHITE COTTON,
SUIT: NAVY COTTON,
BAG: BLACK SHINY
PLASTIC

24
COAT WITH KNIT
COLLAR: BLACK LODEN,
TROUSERS: BLACK
WOOL

25
SHIRT: WHITE COTTON
WITH PLEATED FRONT,
PARKA: BLACK LODEN,
TROUSERS: BLACK
WOOL

01

"Ute and I came up with a very spontaneous approach for the Autumn/Winter 2007/08 'The Messenger' lookbook. The deadline was pretty tight that didn't allow a specific shoot for the looks. Therefore we worked with the show images by Shoji Fujii and thought about a simple but effective way to illustrate the collection's spirit. The shortened pages create a unique, haptic experience. They might be seen as a curtain or a fabric swatch-book, indicating the entirety of the collection and simultaneously depicting each look in itself." Modest in size and production this innovative use of purely functional catwalk photography transformed the conventional into the conceptual.

Lookbooks ROSEBUD INC for UTE PLOIER

1

ONE MAN SHOW

UTE PLOIER
AW 06/07

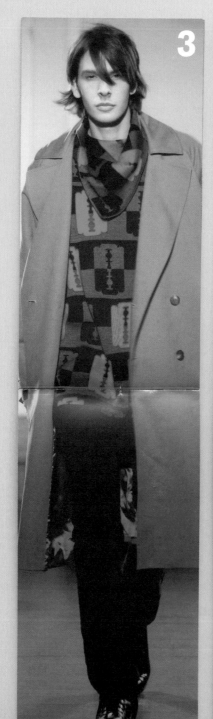

3

6

Inspired by the title of the Autumn/Winter 2006/07 'One Man Show' collection, 'genetic engineering' by Bernd Preiml places the same face onto each of Shoji Fujii's catwalk images. The effect is so perfect that you do not immediately notice.

SO+BA for EDWINA HÖRL

Based within the diverse and creatively vibrant environment of Tokyo, so+ba are Swiss exponents of thorough conceptual process and refined production techniques. Alex Sonderegger and Susanna Baer launched their studio in 2001 with the slogan 'Swiss made in Japan'. After struggling to find satisfaction in their respective places of employment, they had come together to improve their working environment and their final output. As well as being an abbreviation of their surnames, soba is a traditional Japanese noodle and also translates as 'beside/next to', which was appropriate for the partnership they were starting. When they were looking for an office space they discovered a former soba restaurant and could not ignore the serendipity.

Initially drawn to Tokyo through a love of Japanese design, Sonderegger and Baer balance this passion with the lasting influence of their Swiss background and education. While they avoid any obvious house style, a strong conceptual and typographic foundation is tempered by their regular use of illustration. "We examine the product and the company, then collect, hunt, gather visuals and develop various strategies. This information is compiled and distilled into one visual language." While the creative process of so+ba does not exclude moments of intuition, they are predominantly guided by the principle that form follows function.

There is a confident enthusiasm about so+ba that is a result of the intimacy of the founders' partnership. "Our work is like a ping-pong match, or two cooks who try to make one delicious, visual dish! We exchange files regularly at different stages of our work." The seamless quality of this collaboration is extended to client relationships, particularly in the fashion industry. While working with creative clients can be an advantage, so+ba insist that mutual respect is more important to the success of a project.

The fashion designer Edwina Hörl first commissioned so+ba in 2004. Originally from Austria, the label was permanently relocated to Tokyo in 2000. Hörl focuses on the spatial relationships between the body, garments and surrounding environment. Her collections are social indicators of the moment rather than predictions of future trends. Each one is a unique thematic experience that blends contrasting influences with an eclectic range of techniques and materials. With clear creative parallels between Hörl and so+ba, a close collaboration has developed.

The success of the relationship lies in so+ba's ability to extend the central concept of a collection. The lookbooks represent a heightened consideration of this that goes beyond the conventional remit of graphic design. Their first collaboration, for Spring/Summer 2005, was inspired by the children's fable 'The Emperor's New Clothes', which they translated into a poster that showed the garments on one side and the model's body parts on the reverse (see opposite). Their innovative choice of lightweight paper reinforced the theme of the emperor's lack of clothes, pointed out by a small boy in the story: garments and model melded into a single image only when the paper was held to the light. The studio appreciate the creative potential fashion provides for graphic designers, from photography to the catwalk and retail experience, in addition to traditional print requirements. "Working for fashion could be compared to *gesamtkunstwerk* or rather *gesamtdesignwerk*." They believe that participation from the beginning of a collection, while not possible every season, helps to create the perfect working relationship and undoubtedly benefits the results.

The progressive determination of so+ba is illustrated by the words of the Japanese poet Basho: "I do not seek to follow in the footsteps of the men of old. I seek the things they sought." This philosophy helps them to embrace every project as a new challenge. There is an efficiency throughout their process that generates new directions and solutions while maintaining the emphasis on the final result. Their consistent logic and clarity produce the perfect balance between the rational purity of Swiss design and more traditional Japanese aesthetic sensibilities.

www.so-ba.cc
www.edwinahoerl.com

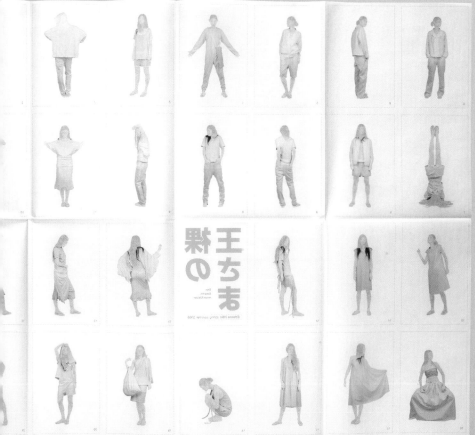

"The Spring/Summer 2005 collection and graphic concept is based on 'Hadaka No Osama' Japanese for the Hans Christian Andersen fable 'The Emperor's New Clothes'. The poster works with the fact that the emperor didn't wear any clothes. On the back only clothes are printed; on the front only the models' body parts. By looking at the poster against the light, the model is visible with the clothes. This was one of our first collaborations with Edwina Hörl so there was some convincing and discussions necessary." Photography by Seiji Shibuya.

Lookbooks SO+BA for EDWINA HÖRL

"The Spring/Summer 2010 'Untitled' lookbook is a multi-cultural reflection on the themes of what makes fashion and clothes. A flea market is a library of worn-already, loved-already clothes. It questions the speed of the never-stopping mainstream fashion market in which nothing is ever new enough. Whether cheap or high-end commodities, all usually reach the flea market sooner or later, enabling this parallel market to survive. We created a booklet with postcard-inlays. The new collection photos in the booklet and the parallel real world flea market photos and inspiration material on the postcards. The cards can fall out when the booklet is opened, creating a chaos similar to the flea market." Photography from the Naschmarkt in Vienna by Jens Preusse, studio photography in Tokyo by Seiji Shibuya.

The Spring/Summer 2008 'Piratery – Garderobbery' lookbook was photographed by Leo Pellegatta. "Piracy: which is an original, which is a copy? Is everything a copy of a copy of a copy? Is culture a big endless copy-machine in which people just re-create? We created a long narrow leporello [a thin, folded sheet of paper] 'harisen' is Japanese for 'slapping fan', when folded it can be use to hit people. On one side all the models and clothes are in a big drunken collage, melting into each other and it is difficult to see the single dresses."

この「無題 / Un-titled チャッシュルクト、ウィーン」というプロジェクトは、ウィーンのナッシュマルクトを利用して「服の中」を、さまざまなポーストスタイルや半分神の服を配し、発見し、識に好きこと、また新しいモードの音楽のインスピレーションとして利用するという二つを主要に引いました「服の中」を、それは永る思考値で使われたもの/がやすでに作る価値で作られた身体価値や価価度では世界を反世界を引き過ぎて人気に取らっまう、場を生類の本体や、さまざまな、デザイナーたちの作品感でもある。

この商売が類されるる「服の中」は、デザイナーたちのある思いでもある。それらは生存を強い、製品はいろコーラの国際でもなしませる。私はのアイデンティティを主張するものは、生まれ持ったと認識されわれている「再保存」そのものやの商価の品位となり、市場に存在する商品の基材となるでしょう。

20世紀以来、ハイ・ファッションにおける建築では、セカンドハンドの態度(De-construction)(Re-construction)が行い。立題がその時代のモード界に出合けました。ようとするたった新運動が又の主産を担める役割によってしまんよとして同じ、さまさまな文化圏とデーでしが含まれます。古価の交換が世界的な器値で行われました。これは半年に変換が切っていっことだけではなく、モードファクンけれがのゆの情のが年起こしきた商もます。

「マルクナフィング、を生活スタイルに付きますものモーグルチャースタイル、これらが自分の報道を「再発展」する世道を二つにしてきる。私はメインストリート、を云るすべにくなると、セカンドハンドの「ヴィンダー」もうとして防御道路で物語ささた流れるよたになり、近代に社界のモードが普ド速度は店まにはエムモデルとなれかみないようになにし。

もちろんにこの共利用/Re-useという想金の根道、品道になったの欲、短事以上の生産を地域を活す生介をする。Re-useは知代のグローバル化物を直がまして、付しい事料の税価を生まましょうます、ブロ化、経費職運動をセカンドハンド新書を使いつ通徹り、生者の産家も報品基の種品はかごとりるものとしてにの運動を持ちまし、それは商用にもした世点の一部所にもある。

「服の中」もより「服価の社分・文化的な報道を反道していてはなりまれん。つまり「服の中」というものかさまざまなものを含まれよんと国際の道のたんして異なる知恵を使わすました「服の中」は、絵的り片段で予備自付別の社会利を世界を生まましょうた。ある時の古日のグループを一家ので用して、のゆり、スタイル(と子の支わ化を手に入れみるものも知わたり、ならこんな新しい価値の音を地出してくれたりる。

SUSAN BARBER for
CHLOË SEVIGNY FOR OPENING CEREMONY

New York City offers Susan Barber a constant source of inspiration and her design process reflects the ebb and flow of the city: "I like to get all the elements together and then think about something else." In these moments of indirect contemplation she finds a creative clarity that refines her subconscious thoughts into reality. For Barber, graphic design is the struggle for balance between elegance and utility, a motivation clearly paralleled in the fashion industry. The continuous creative challenge of fashion together with its diversity gives her a unique sense of satisfaction. "The fashion industry is forward-thinking, always changing and willing to take a chance – all very appealing qualities in a client." This enthusiasm spills out from her studio into her social life as she is more than happy to mix business with pleasure.

In 2005 this resulted in her first commission from friends Carol Lim and Humberto Leon of Opening Ceremony. A multi-faceted brand, Opening Ceremony actively support developing talent through their retail space and showroom. Rather than dictating trends, they encourage individuality and personal interpretation. The foundation of the label is a form of fashion Olympics: every year young designers from the United States are pitted against international opposition. Medals are awarded at the end of the year and the winners are added to Opening Ceremony's roster of designers. Creative collaboration is seen as a key element of the brand's philosophy and a way to continually reinvigorate its message. Chloë Sevigny has produced two collections under the Opening Ceremony banner and is a perfect example of this ongoing commitment.

If collaboration can be translated as confidence in the abilities of others, this was the foundation of the project. "Successful design represents successful collaboration," says Barber. Her experience with Opening Ceremony was so positive that in mid-2009 she was offered a permanent position as their first full-time art director. Her appointment was confirmation of her excellent work and the continued growth of the brand, and a natural decision that will open up a new range of challenges for Barber to take on. It is also confirmation of the positive results that can be achieved when graphic designer and client are united by a common goal and shared aesthetic.

Barber was commissioned to develop the brand's print collateral for the debut Chloë Sevigny For Opening Ceremony Spring/Summer 2008 collection. The lookbook became a focal communication tool, and in true Opening Ceremony style the process of designing it was organic and based on friendship rather than commercial necessity. Sevigny brought in the photographer Mark Borthwick, who has worked with her since she was a teenager, and a host of artists and illustrators to contribute to the lookbook. Although an enormous number of creative people were involved in this single project, the potential for conflict was never realized. "I think it had to do with everyone understanding their role and not trying to go beyond that. On this project specifically it never became an issue, it was a really smooth process."

The lookbook had a mix 'n' match concept that came from one of Sevigny's childhood books and emphasized the interpretative aesthetic and flexibility of the collection. Photographs, illustrations and tinted transparent pages were combined to create endless possibilities. A willingness to obscure details and relinquish control projects a raw aesthetic extension of the collection rather than literal documentation. Barber notes there was a collective enthusiasm for the project that went all the way to the printers. "The thing that makes this book so satisfying is how all the parts work together: the collection, the sublime photography, the eclectic artwork and the unconventional format of the book. All that extra attention added up and the result is like a piece of candy. It's so enticing, anyone who sees this book has to flip through it."

www.susanbarber.com
www.openingceremony.us

The ongoing Chloë Sevigny For Opening Ceremony collaboration was revisited for the Autumn/Winter 2009/10 season. "She invited friends and artists she admired to create artwork that was inspired by redheads. There is also an essay about redheads and all the models had naturally red hair." Photographed by David Armstrong, the cloth-bound hardback achieves a longevity and exclusivity that is quite rare in this context.

AUREL SCHMIDT

KON TRUBKOVICH

ROB PRUITT

"It was a kind of exquisite corpse in book form." Inspired by a children's mix 'n' match book, the Spring/Summer 2008 lookbook was photographed by Mark Borthwick and featured illustrations from a number of artists. "The plastic jacket was a practical choice because we had to have a spiral binding to ensure the book could lay completely flat. I really hate spiral binding on a bookshelf, it looks so messy, but we wanted to show the cover image obviously, so the clear plastic was a way to try and do all those things."

TAKESHI HAMADA for
ADAM ET ROPÉ

Intent on taking full advantage of an increasing number of freelance projects, Takeshi Hamada established his own office in Tokyo in 2003. Predominantly a print-based designer, his refined and intimate creativity concentrates on the subtleties of visual communication. Hamada tries to infuse his work with an artistic sensitivity to balance the commercial requirements of his clients. He admits, "There are always financial obligations but we have to forget this to create something new."

Hamada operates with an introspective confidence in his process. "If I can enjoy it, somebody else can enjoy it too." This produces a very personal body of work that supports the brand message with a unique authenticity. His ability to increase aesthetic value through graphic design is particularly important for the fashion industry. "They want us to create 'beauty' first." More than directly translating a collection, Hamada is able to extend its core narrative through his choice of materials and typographic detailing. In addition to considerable hard work, this requires enormous flexibility given the limited timelines, budgets and variable creative processes of his clients.

Only six months after opening his studio, Hamada was introduced to Adam et Ropé through mutual friends. This casual meeting developed into an ongoing relationship centred on producing the company's seasonal lookbooks. Also based in Japan, Adam et Ropé is a menswear and womenswear label under the Jun Company umbrella. In addition to its mainline collections, it offers a small range of garments and accessories from individually selected labels to enhance the brand experience. While Hamada fulfils the corporate requirements of such a high-volume brand, he has been able to infuse the work with his personal touch.

Although the relationship with Adam et Ropé stretches back many years, Hamada insists that every season presents a fresh set of challenges. While the creative process always starts with the collection, his inspiration comes from the consumer: "Who wears the clothes and what do they feel like?" Rather than seeing fashion as isolated garments on the printed page, he sees it as the covering for the body. This illustrates his broader awareness and the importance he places on functionality in his creative thinking. His subconscious plays an important role, as he absorbs a project's requirements before setting them aside to allow the ideas to flow. "Understand, understand, understand and forget. I cannot get started if I don't forget the analyzed information." While investing heavily in the process, Hamada feels this investment must be balanced by the end result.

For the Spring/Summer 2007 collection, Hamada produced an eight-page mini lookbook in addition to the main catalogue. Without the need for binding, the fragile booklet was covered with a pale green-tinted, wax paper jacket. Always looking to build additional value, Hamada cleverly exploited the translucence of the paper with a hand-drawn, serif title. The well-balanced use of images and materials conveyed a subtle message about the upcoming collection. Hamada believes that in today's world, where information is increasingly available digitally, the materiality of print will grow in value because it directly parallels the physical nature of the human body.

For Hamada, a successful professional relationship must be based on respect in order to build the confidence needed to produce innovative solutions. In time, this develops into mutual trust as both designer and client contribute to the project. "Even if the client has a creative background, it would be difficult to understand each other if they didn't have in trust us." Hamada approaches every project with equal dedication, searching for the creative balance that will satisfy his clients and himself.

www.hamada-takeshi.com
www.adametrope.com

Each lookbook takes advantage of a unique textured cover stock. This attention to the materiality increases the aesthetic value of the experience.

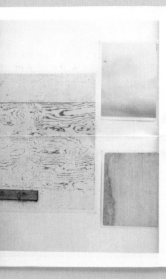

*The mini lookbook for the Spring/
Summer 2007 'Atmosphére' collection
presented an edited selection of images
by Katsuhide Morimoto.*

WILLIAM HALL for
MOTHER OF PEARL

With clinical precision, William Hall concentrates on a refined visual communication. Beyond composition and structure there is a clear, practical interest in how projects feel and are used. Not willing to entertain passing trends, they search for a balance between simplicity and honesty with a rigorous process that justifies every creative decision. This pragmatism provides clear pathways for clients to follow the development and logic of a project. In the pursuit of such clarity all decoration is stripped away; minimal typography and a muted colour palette are often employed to achieve an effortless sophistication.

Motivated by the desire to be responsible for the important decisions on every project, William Hall opened his own studio in London in 2003. Although he is without the security of in-house employment, he is enthused by the potential of dealing directly with clients. "That's when design becomes interesting because you can no longer blame someone else, you're entirely responsible for the result whether it's bad, or good, or brilliant. All our projects have the weight of this possibility now. So the question I ask my colleagues and myself is: 'Is that as good as it can be?'" This continual cycle of refinement is driven by a passion for uncovering a perfect solution.

Hall is unwilling to be distracted by the design press, preferring to maintain creative independence and focus on content to reveal influences that are more relevant to a project. Committed to graphic design as a service, he believes each job must begin and end with the client's brief. This results in a conscious effort to build a diverse portfolio in order to stay creatively fresh. "It's important to avoid slipping into a routine or doing what's expected but nothing more," says Hall. Fashion provides an opportunity to explore more progressive ideas and new production techniques.

The studio's relatively new relationship with Mother of Pearl represents the label's rebirth from an earlier emphasis on beachwear. Its womenswear collection is more relevant to daily life, merging high-tech fabrics with feminine elegance. Hall has built graphic devices to reinforce this new direction, particularly through paper and print finishes. Starting with the Autumn/Winter 2009/10 collection, the invitations and lookbook build a vital link between the texture and materiality of the garments and the print communication. The challenge was to elevate the collection to being something that feels much more expensive and special than it really is."

For Hall, genuine collaboration lies at the heart of an ideal professional relationship. While a creative background can be an advantage, it does not necessarily result in better understanding. Hall presents creative solutions that meet the needs of the client with such clarity that little explanation or debate is required. "More often (though not in the case of Mother of Pearl) the problem is persuading a client to have the confidence to do something with purity." In a world of increasing visual stimulation Hall provides calm and thoughtful alternatives.

Hands-on with every project, Hall also invests a great deal of effort in the non-creative requirements of running the studio. His considered approach to creativity translates to his daily life. "To me the decisions about how I live – the things I touch every day in particular – are important and contribute to my quality of life. I feel the same way about clothes."

www.williamhall.co.uk
www.motherofpearl.co.uk

"The Autumn/Winter 2009/10 lookbook is elevated by two main devices – the use of an embossed, gridded paper for the cover, and an inline varnish that runs on all the image spreads. We arranged the collection into three groups: signature pieces, evening wear and everything else, then we gave each group its own type of varnish. So you're assisted in a very subtle way in understanding the collection. The varnishes also add some complexity and dynamism." The subtle detail of gold staples is only revealed on the centrefold as the spine is bound with white textured tape. The photography was by Andrew Woffinden.

"Mother of Pearl don't have a catwalk show, so the lookbook is a key promotional tool. It has to provide all the texture, drama and colour usually witnessed on the catwalk. As well as communicating the collection, it is also an expression of the brand itself. The Spring/Summer 2010 collection took a modernist direction with clean lines and drama provided via prints from YBA Mat Collishaw. We created a series of interior/exterior spaces from a very limited palette of grey and gold walls. Tim Gutt's elegant and resonant images feature a refined and stable environment into which the model and her clothes provide all the colour and energy. The lookbook itself uses high-quality materials and complex finishing, which again reflect the preoccupations of the Mother of Pearl brand. The cover echoes the invitation we made for the launch of the collection. The invitation combines a standard hangtag with a purpose-made, burgundy A6 invitation card. Carrying this through to the lookbook made a strong association throughout the collection." The lookbooks were designed with Laura Tabet.*

Mother of Pearl
Spring Summer 2010

Lookbooks GRAPHIC DESIGN for FASHION

PACKAGING

**IS PRIMARILY
USED TO HOLD AND
PROTECT PRODUCTS
WHEN ON DISPLAY
OR AFTER PURCHASE.
IT PROVIDES AN
ADDITIONAL CREATIVE
OUTLET TO EXTEND THE
BRAND EXPERIENCE.**

INTRODUCTION

COMPLEMENTARY TO THE PRODUCT, PACKAGING CAN ENHANCE THE CONSUMER EXPERIENCE IN A UNIQUE WAY. MORE THAN A SIMPLE CONTAINER, IT CAN BE SEEN AS THE CULMINATION OF THE LABEL'S VISUAL COMMUNICATION, IMPRINTING A LASTING MESSAGE OF AESTHETIC VALUE. THE DESIGNER IS ASKED TO PRODUCE A SOLUTION THAT IS APPLICABLE TO THE ESTABLISHED CREATIVE AESTHETIC YET POTENTIALLY BROAD ENOUGH TO BE RELEVANT IN FUTURE SEASONS, ALL ACHIEVED WITHIN A BUDGET THAT ALLOWS THE PACKAGING TO BE GIVEN AWAY FOR FREE.

THE HIGH STREET IS FLOODED WITH BRANDED SHOPPING BAGS. THE FASHION LABELS ACKNOWLEDGE THE PROMOTIONAL POTENTIAL AND THE CONSUMER IS HAPPY TO PUBLICALLY PROFESS THEIR ALLEGIANCE AND PROMOTE THE MESSAGE OF ASPIRATION. IT IS AN ACTIVE RELATIONSHIP. A COMBINATION OF POWERFUL BRAND ASSOCIATION AND WELL-EXECUTED DESIGN, PACKAGING SOLUTIONS ARE FAR FROM DISPOSABLE.

HOW DO YOU KNOW WHEN SOMETHING IS GOOD? ACCUMULATION OF THE MEMORY[226] IT HAS A LOT TO DO WITH INTUITION, OF COURSE THAT THE CLIENT IS HAPPY AND OBVIOUSLY THAT EXTRA JOY AND KICK IN RAPTURE, WHEN YOU JUST KNOW THAT SOMETHING IS RIGHT AT THE VERY MOMENT[228] IT'S A COMPLETE VISUAL PACKAGE. IT LOOKS GREAT, WELL CONSIDERED AND EXECUTED, BUT ALSO IT COMES ACROSS AS SUCCESSFUL FROM THE CLIENT SIDE, COMMUNICATING THE BRAND AND HELPS THEM BE DISTINCTIVE FROM THEIR COMPETITORS[232] WHEN IT MAKES ME HAPPY LOOKING AT IT; WHEN IT'S HONEST AND NOT OVERLY COMPLICATED; WHEN I HAVEN'T SEEN IT BEFORE; WHEN I HAVE A CERTAIN CONFIDENCE THAT IT WILL ALSO WORK WELL FOR THE CLIENT[236] IF I LOOK AT THE PROJECT A YEAR AFTER AND I THINK TO MYSELF "I LIKE THAT".[238]

ARTLESS for ISSEY MIYAKE

Artless is a creative collective based in Tokyo. Established by Shun Kawakami in 2000 as the commercial vehicle for his creative output, it upholds "design as a visual language" with the conscious intention to bridge the gap between "art and design". Flexibility is vital to its structure as Kawakami is able to draft in specific collaborators to fulfil his vision for each project, moving between art, print and interaction design with ease. Inspired by traditional Japanese craft such as flower arranging, bonsai and calligraphy, Kawakami is dedicated to translating his national identity into the modern creative context. He is motivated by the varied impressions this culturally driven aesthetic leaves on an international audience. As an exercise in refined balance, the results are innovative and appeal to a broad range of people.

Kawakami thrives on the fashion industry's continuous demands for creative innovation and high production values. A natural enthusiasm for its products and respect for how they are created stimulates his interest in fashion. "I think fashion affects the mind of the individual." This personal connection motivates his creativity as he is simultaneously designer and audience. "Maybe... I sympathize with their creative sensitivity." Engaged with the product and always investing personally in a project, Kawakami offers his clients wide-ranging expertise, from an independent perspective. "I think the graphic designer needs to be a doctor, translator and chef."

Established in 1970, Issey Miyake has remained at the forefront of progressive fashion design through the refined simplicity of his silhouette, which blends function with contemporary technological innovation. Research, experimentation and development have been vital features of his success and are equally important in Artless's practice. While their disciplines are separate, this similarity of creative process provides immediate common ground between client and designer. Initially briefed for the redesign of the Issey Miyake website in 2006 – Kawakami's strong understanding of the core values of the label has seen his involvement increase.

After the original commission, it was a logical extension for Artless to develop a range of packaging unique to the online shopping experience. Kawakami admits to being offered limited instructions that amounted to a purely functional requirement: "The brief was very simple, to use www.isseymiyake.com." With the mutual confidence engendered by an established relationship, Kawakami was granted complete creative freedom to interpret the challenge. With a natural ability to refine the message, Kawakami transformed the structure of the domain into the central concept. The innovative typographic treatment is, in fact, derived from the punctuation marks and slashes associated with web domains. The appropriation of this onto raw, corrugated cardboard reinforces the pure, functional aesthetic of the concept.

For Kawakami, intuition plays an important part in his process; spontaneous moments of inspiration drive the direction of his projects in a practical way. He looks for new connections and interchanges between his interests and those of collaborators and clients. He believes his role as designer is to interpret the creative thoughts of his clients. Rather than collaborating conventionally, he takes responsibility for what he does, and responds best when he is granted the freedom to explore his own interpretation of the task in hand. Personally engaged with his work, in his practice Kawakami attempts to achieve a sense of longevity that extends beyond seasonal trends.

www.artless.co.jp
www.isseymiyake.com

To cater for potential variation in size of each order the boxes were produced in three sizes.

HOMEWORK for FLEUR TANG

With a natural affinity for "double-acting words" and the simple fact that he initially was combining 'home' and 'work', in 2002 Jack Dahl set up Homework in Copenhagen. He insists the name relates equally to his practice and his clients as each party in the relationship has certain responsibilities and must do 'homework' in order to maximize a project's potential. In particular, the implication that education is continued beyond professional life is appropriate, supporting his belief that "there is so much more to learn in life and through personal developments; philosophical, spiritual and psychological". With his enthusiasm for self-improvement, he has maintained a youthful passion for design while building a well-respected creative studio.

Homework have a clean and classical style, which is also contemporary and abstract. This aesthetic has been used with great success in progressive fashion magazines. Bold typography, colour and photography express the confidence in attitude and direction that drives Homework. While he flirts with the balance of creativity and commercial viability, Dahl remains focused on the unique requirements of each project. "It's not always about creating a completely new solution, but maybe more about trying to make something ordinary feel tempting and look interesting." This ability to extract nuanced details allows the work of Homework to be comfortable yet progressive.

Although they are entrusted with large-scale projects, Homework have remained a modest size, and deliberately avoid layers of management. Dedicated to implementing designs personally, Dahl is completely hands-on. "If the project and the client's dreams, beliefs and personality are interesting, it excites me." His passion for creativity is infectious and draws clients directly into the design process.

Dahl appreciates that when working for the fashion industry the results can be spectacular, but admits there are no guarantees. "I prefer collaborations defined by mutual respect and based on similar ideals and perhaps, but not necessarily, aesthetics." Since 2007, Homework have provided all the visual communication for Fleur Tang in what has become a very close relationship. There is an ease of communication that has more in common with friendship than with a commercial partnership, and strengthens over time. While each has unique responsibilities, the end result is a true collaboration.

Mutual enthusiasm for the product lies at the heart of the relationship. Fleur Tang is an ethical range of basic clothing, produced with 100 per cent organic cotton, that supports a strong environmental message which is imposed at every stage of the creative and manufacturing process. While they follow the fashion seasons, the collection is limited and only minimal additions are made. "The brief and goal was to discover a new, fresh but understated organic packaging," says Dahl. Difficult to source in a suitable colour and quality, sustainable, raw card was the material of choice. Focusing on the materiality of the product and packaging, blind embossing of the logo was an ideal solution because of the low environmental impact. In addition, working with local packaging manufacturers, different ways of closing the boxes were explored to build on the complexity and originality of the overall aesthetic. Practical in function, yet refined to touch, the packaging represents a truly cohesive brand communication.

"Fleur Tang garments and packaging are made with 100 per cent organic materials. From the cotton in the mills to the manufacturing, every process is done with the environment in mind – and without harmful chemicals. A piece of clothing with peace of mind." The minimal design aesthetic features a single logo embossed onto each package. Substantial effort was invested in developing an innovative closure for the box to enhance the uniqueness of the experience.

www.homework.dk
www.fleurtang.com

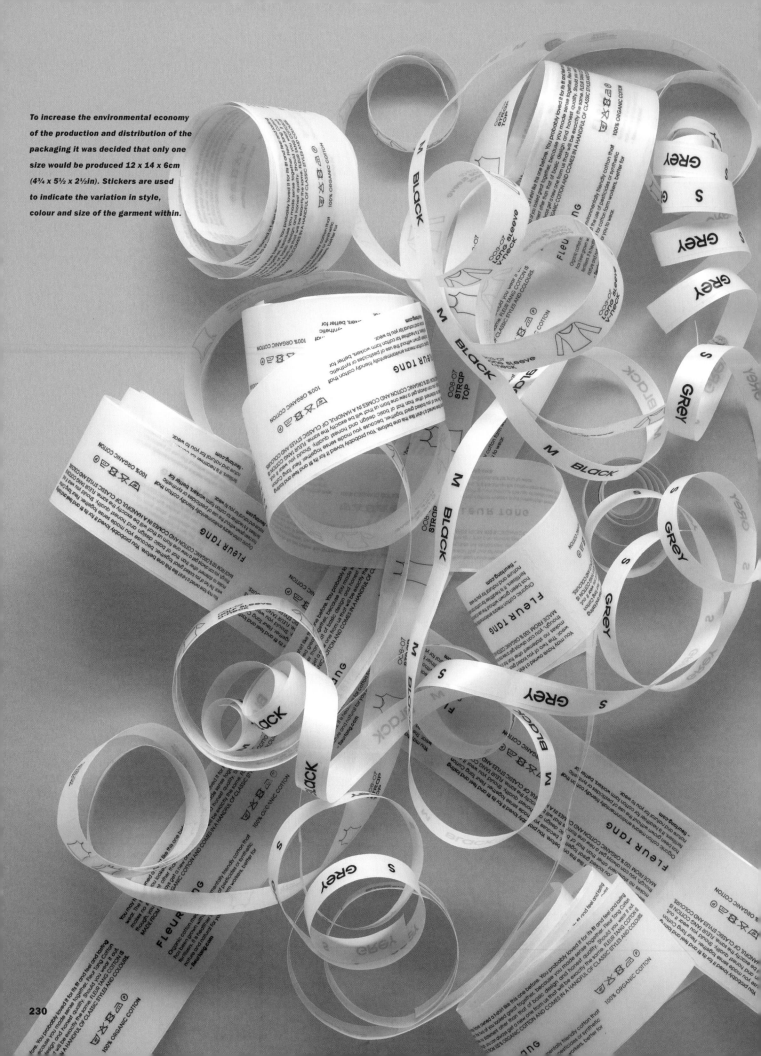

To increase the environmental economy of the production and distribution of the packaging it was decided that only one size would be produced 12 x 14 x 6cm (4¾ x 5½ x 2½in). Stickers are used to indicate the variation in style, colour and size of the garment within.

*Due to the raw quality of the card, subtle
tonal variations may appear in different
batches of the packaging. Display cases
were created in two sizes by Suthi Tang,
using the same materials as the
packaging, but in contrasting colours.*

Packaging HOMEWORK for FLEUR TANG

MARQUE CREATIVE for
VÍCTOR ALFARO

Marque have offices in London, New York and Glasgow, but distance is no obstacle to creativity as the company maintains a collective work ethic in all its projects. As a branding consultancy, this geographical spread creates an important social and cultural pool from which to draw inspiration. Its head office is in Glasgow, where it first opened its doors in 1994 as Third Eye Design. As the services the company now provides evolved, in mid-2008 it was rebranded as Marque Creative, a reference to its increased focus on branding and a subtle play on the name of the agency founder and managing director: Mark Noë.

In 2007 the New York office won the contract to complete the brand identity and packaging for a new luxury womenswear line by Víctor Alfaro. Also based in New York, Alfaro rose to fame in the early 1990s with body-conscious silhouettes and luxurious materials that projected the refined simplicity of feminine beauty. After stepping away from the fashion industry for a few years, he returned to produce Víctor for Víctor Alfaro exclusively for the American retail store Bon-Ton. Importantly, Alfaro insisted on bringing in Marque to ensure the visual communication would match the high standards he sets for the garments. "Víctor was very eager to make something luxurious out of the project," says the current director Lisa Smith.

Marque begin all new projects with a 'branding workshop' with the client. Alfaro's participation in the brainstorming session immediately established a sense of collective ownership over the creative process and provided vital information to shape the future direction. Importantly, the agency and client always produce the brief together to ensure the final product meets all expectations. Regardless of the client's creative capability, the initial collaborative exploration is a trademark of Marque's highly effective, structured practice.

This refined approach is continued throughout their collaboration with Alfaro; ideas are never just a scribble on a napkin. "Every stage is very engineered, right from the beginning," says Smith. This is particularly important because of the amount of work the project requires and its logistical complexity. Smith notes that while working for the fashion industry can clearly drive creative innovation, practical concerns and compromise ultimately affect the end product. Marque are responsible for finding the balance between Alfaro's aesthetic demands and the financial obligations associated with Bon-Ton's commercial investment.

The packaging is a direct extension of the branding of the label with heavy use of the VA logomark pattern. Modern, and edgy yet accessible, there is a retro feel to the letterform and colour palette. Research into materials was exhaustive as Marque sought to make their presentations as practical as possible. "We did rubdowns, made labels and showed many samples of papers and materials. Víctor is very visual and needs that level of service. He needs to see and feel what he is getting." The success of the project can be measured by the use of the VA logomark throughout the collection: buttons, denim back pockets, zippers, closures and handbag linings.

Marque are somewhat rare in that they are a global agency with a personal touch. Through their refined creative process and continual internal dialogue they achieve a high level of flexibility to satisfy their broad client base. "You approach fashion the same way you approach every client, with the same level of detail that you want to bring to the project," says Smith. She maintains that it is important to focus on a client's requirements and not be distracted by trends and peer approval. Marque produce a body of work that adheres to this belief, but nevertheless consistently insert intimate moments of inspiration.

An example of a jewellery box for necklaces and bracelets that was produced in three different sizes.

www.marquecreative.com

Packaging MARQUE CREATIVE for VÍCTOR ALFARO

The Víctor Alfaro shoe range features complementary casual and luxury collections. To emphasize this distinction two independent shoebox designs were produced. Each line required ballet-, regular- and boot-sized boxes.

OPPOSITE : "This VA repeat pattern adds a textural quality, whether through debossing, spot varnishes or as full colour with a matt bronze streak through it on the packaging. Rich, earthy colourways – brown self-coloured stocks and bronze foil detailing – work with the sumptuousness of the materials used in his collections."

VÍCTOR
VÍCTOR ALFARO

VÍCTOR

VÍCTOR
VÍCTOR ALFARO

Packaging MARQUE CREATIVE for VÍCTOR ALFARO

MIND DESIGN for
LACOSTE BY TOM DIXON

The conceptual rigour behind the work of London-based Mind Design is balanced by an emphasis on flexible creative solutions. Dedicated to the integration of a central idea over a range of applications, the studio fight the static restrictions of print with subtle variations. Its approach is immediately accessible yet is always justified with deeper consideration. In contrast to corporate studio structure, Mind Design benefits from an individuality and spontaneity that is maintained throughout every project.

After graduation Holger Jacobs accepted an opportunity to work in Japan, an experience that continues to have a strong influence on his work. From this different cultural perspective he developed a deeper understanding of Western typography. When he returned to London in 1999 he started Mind Design as a short-term requirement of being self-employed. The studio name draws on his interest in visual poetry and word games, yet Jacobs insists it was more of an accident. "We actually never liked the name very much as it sounds a bit too clever," he says. Mind has grown steadily – care was taken to ensure that expansion did not damage the intimacy of its process – and now has five designers.

While it is enthusiastically creative, Mind does not lose sight of the commercial realities of its role. "Design is not art. It is usually commissioned and has a certain purpose," says Jacobs. The ability to articulate its process creates clarity within the studio and confidence in its clients. A foundation for all relationships, this helps to build the mutual respect necessary to establish a creative

partnership with each project. There is a pursuit of a personal connection with their work that draws upon individual emotional and often quite random influences. "Something that I see on the street can lead to a great idea; if I cycled down a different street I might have had a different idea. I don't really believe in step-by-step analytical concept development any more and don't think there is only one best 'solution' in design." Jacobs is interested in the creative process, but remains conscious of what is required technically to avoid last-minute compromises. There is a strong emphasis on craftsmanship and production in every stage of development.

Jacobs appreciates the relative glamour of working for the fashion industry, yet feels the creative challenge is somewhat reduced when working with an immediately appealing product. He sees the borders between fashion and other arenas becoming more blurred in modern society. This is evident in the initiative by LACOSTE, who each year invite a designer from outside the industry to reinterpret their classic polo shirt and challenge their production methods and processes. The iconic French sportswear label, which has built its reputation on comfort, quality and engineering textiles for enhanced performance, continues to pursue creative innovation.

In 2006, Tom Dixon was the first designer to collaborate with LACOSTE on their Holiday Collector's Series. Recognized as a leading figure in furniture, lighting and product design, Dixon is known for his use of raw materials and infusing narrative into his work. Exploring the tension between ecology and technology,

the results for LACOSTE clarified the parallels between the company's heritage and Dixon's own influences. Two contrasting yet complementary shirts were produced: Eco Polo and Techno Polo (see opposite).

Mind enjoy a close collaboration with Dixon through regular commissions and was involved from the outset of the project. They share a mutual interest in incorporating the production process as part of the design, and this undoubtedly influenced the end results. The near-symmetrical typographic treatment clarifies the similarity of the shirts while contrasting materials reaffirm their individuality. Because this was a limited-edition project the usual concerns of longevity and brand integration were not relevant, which allowed the design to be informed exclusively by content. Beyond the packaging the collaboration covered label tags and specially commissioned, hand-painted promotional graphics for the product launch.

While the shared creative background of the fashion industry can be an advantage, Jacobs is philosophical about generalizing. "I have met fashion designers with very specific ideas of what they want, who just needed a graphic designer for the execution. On the other hand, fashion clients can be very open to unusual ideas and really understand the importance of quality printing." For him, the success of a relationship relies on constructive dialogue and compatible sensibilities. He is confident that with this process creative solutions simply fall into place.

www.minddesign.co.uk
www.lacoste.com
www.tomdixon.net

"Tom had a large influence on the design of the packaging but gave us total freedom in the actual graphics and typography. For the Eco Polo we did not want to use any printing on the packaging and labels at all, so the design was embossed into a recycled, egg carton-like material. For the Techno Polo Tom suggested a silver, vacuum-packed foil packaging that was screen-printed. On the matching labels we worked with silver foil blocking. Originally we wanted to produce a talking electronic price tag, which became too difficult to realize. Since the Eco Polo was hand-dyed in India we work with a group of Bollywood artists for the launch graphics. Based on our research into this particular style, we designed three collages as templates for the artists. They were then e-mailed to India, hand-painted on a large format canvas to be shown at Dover Street Market in London... In this instance the process was almost more important than the actual results. The product really is a story of the process and it was an important part of our design to tell the story."

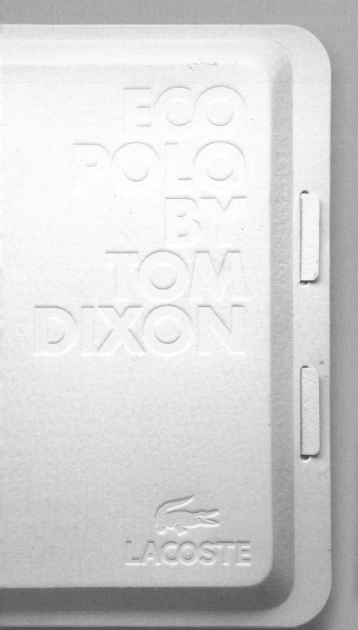

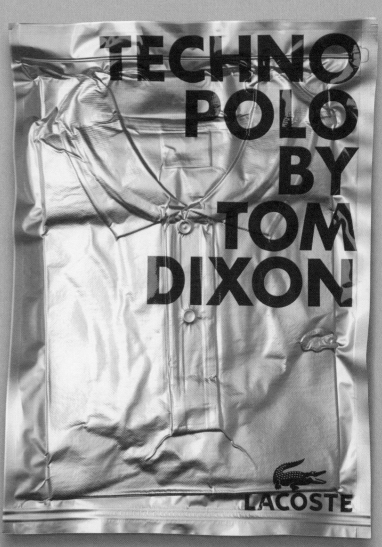

THORBJØRN ANKERSTJERNE
for QASIMI

Enthusiasm is not something Thorbjørn Ankerstjerne lacks. He infuses all his work with passion and a personal commitment that goes beyond conventional expectations: "I think it is very important to get excited about what you do." Creative ownership is vital, as he takes responsibility to push a project as far as possible. Constructive and honest communication with clients is required to streamline the design process and facilitate his free-flowing ideas. His relocation from Copenhagen to London in 2007 has opened up an increasingly diverse range of projects as he moves from graphic design as a corporate application to "a device that can work in a cultural context".

Respectful of the challenge to "portray someone's collections and thoughts with a piece of graphic design", Ankerstjerne thrives on the seasonal nature and speed of the fashion industry. The urgency seems to stimulate his creativity and was one of his strengths when Qasimi commissioned him to complete the groundwork of a rebrand within a few weeks. Qasimi were familiar with his earlier work and believed that his visual aesthetic would enable him to interpret their brand in this short period of time. Ankerstjerne enlisted Fabio Sebastianelli as a collaborator and immediately got to work setting out the framework for the project. "We had a very clear idea what we wanted from the beginning – to be very clean, simple, classic and something we could adapt to their men's and women's collections." This rationale directly reflects the luxurious fabrics and sophistication of the Qasimi brand.

For Ankerstjerne, a successful relationship is about open dialogue and he relies on his clients to participate constructively to resolve problems. "If the collaboration is really working well, the more integrated you can become in their thinking and the better results you can produce. You can start to feel what they want more, and can twist it more."

Ankerstjerne can be vigorous in defence of his concepts if he believes this will benefit a project, but is able to temper this passion and work through problems to find new solutions that are mutually satisfying. He maintains extremely high standards for every stage of the design process. "I feel really strongly about quality and want my work to be seen in the best way possible. It does not take a lot to ruin something, but it is also pretty easy to make something good. It is just about making people aware of that." The ability to rationalize his creative process is a great advantage as he strives to justify his decisions and, most importantly, infect others with his passion for design.

Ankerstjerne was free to create a completely new look and feel for the brand communication without any reference to the previous logo. Doing this became an exercise in reduction; by literally removing all extraneous elements from the letterforms the breakthrough came with the development of an abstract geometric pattern. This was initially presented to Qasimi as a motion sequence, to emphasize the flexibility of the concept and that it was more than a mark. Materiality always plays a central role in Ankerstjerne's work and he quickly realized the potential of the pattern, particularly for the packaging.

The shopping bag succeeds because of Ankerstjerne's innovative understanding of its material qualities. Its conventional structure is enhanced when, in the right light, the paper becomes translucent and reveals the inner pattern on the otherwise plain exterior – almost magical in its simplicity, this subtle effect showcases Ankerstjerne's understated touch. A tribute to the success of the pattern is that it has become central to Qasimi's branding and they infuse it back into their collections on garments, linings, prints, boots and even jewellery. Although it was initially used to complete a graphic design project, it has expanded beyond the usual parameters and directly informs fashion in what has become a continuous loop. It is continually progressive, with the ability to adjust specifically to each collection. "For something so simple it is really fortunate to create a mark that is so flexible," says Ankerstjerne.

www.ankerstjerne.co.uk
www.qasimi.com

*Only produced in a standard size,
when the bag catches the light from
the right angle, it reveals the pattern
on the clean, white exterior. The optical
illusion is achieved by printing an
inverse pattern on the inside of the bag.
"There are a million different ways to
work with the pattern," says Ankerstjerne.*

Packaging THORBJØRN ANKERSTJERNE for QASIMI